Preparing a Professional Portfolio

A School Administrator's Guide

Bradley V. Balch

Indiana State University

Pamela M. Frampton

Purdue University, Calumet

Marilyn A. Hirth

Purdue University

PEARSON

Boston   New York   San Francisco
Mexico City   Montreal   Toronto   London   Madrid   Munich   Paris
Hong Kong   Singapore   Tokyo   Cape Town   Sydney

Senior Editor: *Arnis E. Burvikovs*
Editorial Assistant: *Kelly Hopkins*
Marketing Manager: *Tara Kelly*
Production Editor: *Greg Erb*
Editorial Production Service: *Publishers' Design and Production Services, Inc.*
Composition and Manufacturing Buyer: *Andrew Turso*
Electronic Composition: *Publishers' Design and Production Services, Inc.*
Cover Designer: *Joel Gendron*

For related titles and support materials, visit our online catalog at www.ablongman.com.

Between the time website information is gathered and then published, it is not unusual for some sites to have closed. Also, the transcription of URLs can result in typographical errors. The publisher would appreciate notification where these errors occur so that they may be corrected in subsequent editions.

Library of Congress Cataloging-in-Publication Data
Balch, Bradley V.
    Preparing a professional portfolio : a school administrator's guide / Bradley V. Balch, Pamela M. Frampton, Marilyn A. Hirth.
        p. cm.
    Includes bibliographical references and index.
    ISBN 0-205-46720-2 (alk. paper)
        1. School administrators—United States—Evaluation—Handbooks, manuals, etc. 2. School administrators—Certification—United States—Handbooks, manuals, etc. 3. School administrators—Selection and appointment—United States—Handbooks, manuals, etc. 4. Portfolios in education—United States—Handbooks, manuals, etc. I. Frampton, Pamela M. II. Hirth, Marilyn A. III. Title.
    LB2831.82.F73 2006   2005045900
    371.2'011—dc22

Printed in the United States of America

10 9 8 7 6 5 4 3 2 1   HAM   09 08 07 06 05

CONTENTS

PREFACE

The Interstate School Leaders Licensure Consortium (ISLLC) standards have challenged administration preparation programs to provide capacities for student assistance in understanding the national standards as well as to operationalize them through administrative practices. In addition, school leaders and institutions of higher education are searching for resources concerning portfolio development based on standards.

This book fills a serious void with regard to information and guidelines on portfolios and standards-based licensing requirements for both building-level and district-level administrators. It can be used as a supportive text in administrative courses or as a guide for independent study courses. Furthermore, this book will assist the reader in developing a meaningful standards-based portfolio, at the same time exploring the changing views of school leadership. An increasing number of districts are requiring the use of portfolios as a vehicle toward professional growth. In some cases, building and district administrators are required to develop professional portfolios to satisfy evaluation expectations.

This book is also useful for practicing school leaders pursuing licensure renewal and for aspiring leaders building job placement credentials. A reflective, standards-based portfolio is especially helpful to candidates seeking new positions. Such a portfolio can be made available electronically by posting it online, providing it as a CD to a potential employer, or presenting it in hard-copy form. Not only does this book guide the reader in the development and completion of a meaningful portfolio, but it also presents enhanced explanations of each of the ISLLC standards so that the reader can find meaning in the standards and implement them in authentic ways. Each chapter of the book will include the following: (1) an explanation of the standard, emphasizing key components and further direction for implementing the standard in practice; (2) suggestions for appropriate portfolio development; (3) ideas for portfolio artifacts and narratives; and, lastly, (4) a sample portfolio entry and case study for the standard. An entire presentation of the standards is found in Appendix A. The standards are organized conceptually by performances, knowledges, and dispositions (i.e., attitudes). Two additional standards are introduced in this book that are specific to district-level leadership. Although these standards have been adopted and fully codified in the state of Indiana, they are representative of other states (e.g., Michigan) that have identified their own unique standards-based outcomes not specifically manifested in an ISLLC standard. When appropriate, the reader is encouraged to adopt this book's easy-to-follow template for understanding and operationalizing standards other than the ISLLC standards.

Background of Portfolios and School Leader Licensure

The National Board for Professional Teaching Standards (NBPTS) originally fostered the idea of using professional portfolios as a means of assessing and granting National Board status for teachers based on their performance. This work, led by Linda Darling–Hammond, first looked at identifying what it means to be an effective teacher—no small task by far. Feedback from teachers and other educators further helped to create a substantial framework informed by using five core areas of **assessment** as a means to guide the teaching profession. These NBPTS **standards** measure a teacher's practice using portfolios, classroom videotapes, and student work samples as a means to analyze classroom teaching and student learning. In addition to the performance-based assessments, teachers also complete written exercises intended to test their content knowledge and understanding.

Using the conceptual framework of the NBPTS standards as a guide, the Interstate School Leaders Licensure Consortium (ISLLC) initiative prompted individual states to begin similar performance-based assessments of administrators. Established in 1994, the ISLLC was a consortium of 45 different agencies, serving as stakeholders of education and educational administration. These diverse agencies worked cooperatively to establish a school leader's conceptual framework for policy and assessment. The ISLLC's vision of leadership was based on the belief that standards for a school leader's practice must be immersed in an understanding of teaching and learning. Using the ISLLC guidelines, individual states could work together to develop model standards, assessments, professional development, and licensing procedures, thus effectively helping to recruit, prepare, and retain better, more capable, educational administrators. Table 1 summarizes the ISLLC standards.

The Developmental Nature of the Standards

As school administrators develop their professional identity, attempting to be all-things-to-all-people is a common first step, soon replaced by the unique leadership gifts and talents inherent to the leader. Likewise, as school administrators begin a path to professional maturity, it is too often assumed that standards are a list of essential skills that must be fully attained as soon as possible. On the contrary, standards are a listing of developmental performances, knowledges, and dispositions that are attained throughout a lifetime of professional service. There are five distinct phases of standards attainment that guide administrative practice.

Phase 1: Introductory

Aspiring administrators begin a foundational phase with regard to standards. During this period of their development they gain insight into the standards' meaning while forming foundational understandings of how the varying components of the standards might be demonstrated. For example, in ISLLC Standard 1, a student might focus on only two or three performances, knowledges, and dispositions, and may complete a task that demonstrates an understanding of these components. The student may also complete a project such as a shadow study of a practicing administrator in which there is a brief literature reference to the knowledges associated with vision, a description of the performances for ISLLC Standard 1 as demonstrated by the practicing school leader being shadowed, and a personal reflection section in which the student discusses the dispositions regarding the standard and any personal reaction to them.

TABLE 1   Summary of Standards

Standard	Knowledges	Dispositions	Performances
1: A Vision of Learning	■ Pluralistic society ■ Educational leadership theories ■ Data collection and analysis	■ Educability of all ■ Ideal of the common good ■ High standards of learning ■ Inclusion of all stakeholders	■ Model core beliefs ■ Developing and monitoring shared vision ■ Strategic planning ■ Data collection and analysis
2: School Culture and Instructional Program	■ School culture ■ Student growth and development ■ Applied learning theories ■ Adult learning and professional development	■ Student learning is fundamental purpose ■ All students can learn ■ Lifelong learning ■ Safe and supportive learning environment	■ Treat all with fairness, dignity, respect ■ Recognize student and staff accomplishments ■ Variety of supervisory and evaluation models ■ Multiple opportunities to learn ■ Culture and climate assessed regularly
3: Management	■ Principles of organizational development ■ Human resources management and development ■ School safety and security ■ Fiscal management ■ Facilities management	■ Management decisions enhance learning ■ Trusting people ■ Accepting responsibility ■ Involving stakeholders	■ Procedures optimize successful learning ■ Operational plans in place ■ Effectively manage collective bargaining ■ Conflict is managed
4: Collaboration with Families and the Community	■ Emerging issues and trends ■ Community diversity ■ Community resources ■ Partnership models	■ Collaboration and communication ■ Families as partners ■ Informing the public ■ Diversity can enrich the school	■ High visibility and communication ■ Outreach evidence ■ Equitable treatment of stakeholders ■ Effective media relations ■ Multicultural awareness and sensitivity

(continued)

TABLE 1   Continued

Standard	Knowledges	Dispositions	Performances
5: Acting with Integrity and Fairness, and in an Ethical Manner	■ Purpose and role of education and leadership ■ Values, ethics, challenges of diverse community ■ Professional code of ethics	■ Ideal of the common good ■ Principles of the Bill of Rights ■ Ethics in decision making ■ A caring culture	■ Demonstrates personal/professional code ■ Accepts responsibility ■ Treats people fairly, equitably, and with dignity ■ Fulfills legal and contractual obligations ■ Protects rights and confidentiality
6: The Political, Social, Economic, Legal, and Cultural Context	■ Principles of representative government ■ Role of public education ■ Education and school law ■ Global issues	■ Education is a key to opportunity ■ Recognizing a variety of ideas, values, cultures ■ Active participation in policy making ■ Using legal system to protect students	■ Communications regarding trends, issues ■ Shapes public policy for quality education ■ Communicates with decision makers
7: Instructional Program (as used in Indiana)	■ Carefully align the curriculum to meet the needs of the broader, diverse community ■ Using appropriate assessment, determine the equitability, effectiveness, and relevance of the instructional program	■ Understanding of the developmental needs of students from pre-K to after high school ■ Understanding of projected strategic planning utilizing data to foresee district needs ■ Understanding the use of technology and its relevance to school planning	■ Appreciation for the diversity of the community and its importance in instructional planning ■ Use of technology to enhance instruction ■ Use of multiple assessment techniques to improve the instructional program
8: Policy Implementation (as used in Indiana)	■ Compliance with state, federal, and local laws ■ Positive relationships with school board ■ Make and communicate policy	■ Understanding of public school governance ■ Understanding of conflict resolution and sound policy making ■ Principles of law, civil and criminal liability	■ Works within laws of state, federal, and local governance ■ Supports school system ■ Creates educational opportunities for all in the community

Phase 2: Developmental

Phase 2 is a period during which the aspiring leader is completing the initial coursework and beginning a formal or informal induction period into school leadership. During this phase, an emerging administrator will transition into a deeper understanding of standards and will demonstrate some success in the attainment of the standards. For example, a newly hired administrator might work on ISLLC Standard 1 with the following portfolio entry:

1. Selection of an activity that is embedded in the school day, such as working with a grade-level team at a middle school to monitor the implementation of the school's vision
2. An audio- or videotape of a representative meeting during which the new administrator attempts to facilitate team consensus
3. An analysis of the tape through a process of narrative, including a rationale statement explaining why the artifact was chosen and how it relates to Standard 1, a description of the session (e.g., who is involved, purpose of the meeting, etc.), an analysis of what occurred during the taping of the meeting, and finally a reflection on how the administrator might improve on the results if the process could be repeated

This developmental phase implies that the leader has more than a cursory understanding of the standards and is beginning to put performances, knowledges, and dispositions into authentic practice.

Phase 3: Proficiency

During the proficiency phase, the school leader has mastered the basic components of the standards and is beginning to see a level of attainment beyond the first two phases of introduction and development. For example, a leader in the proficiency phase has completed approximately five years or more of administrative practice and is beginning to show expertise in all ISLLC standards. A proficient leader consistently performs the actions associated with all six standards, demonstrates a keen understanding of the knowledges of each standard, and articulates the appropriate dispositions in all phases of the job.

Phase 4: Maintenance and Renewal

The fourth stage, maintenance and renewal, includes a high level of expertise and activities related to maintaining and renewing administrative practices. During this phase, the leader has approximately 10 years or more of administrative practice and can evidence numerous examples of standards attainment. Phase 4 is a time when the leader seeks renewal by serving the larger community of leaders through various activities, including membership on community and professional boards; advising; supervising and teaching in preparation programs; presenting at national, state, and regional conferences; and, most important, serving as a mentor for novice administrators. During the maintenance and renewal phase, the leader leverages experience to help recruit, retain, and socialize a new generation of school administrators.

Phase 5: Assessment

As school leaders near the apex of their careers, they begin to take on a new role with regard to standards—the role of the assessor. At this stage, master administrators call on their vast experiences in leading schools to give back to their profession, in part through the *assessment* of evidence related to standards and portfolios. Additionally, they use their talents and wisdom to mentor novice school leaders, and to retain and socialize them in practice.

In summary, the standards are not a static set of items from a banal checklist, but rather are a dynamic and developmental set of constructs that will guide school leaders from their beginning days to their final days in school administration. It is vitally important that preparation programs develop expectations that reflect the developmental nature of the school leader standards. Additionally, state licensing frameworks should reflect an understanding of the differing phases of attainment. The professional portfolio of a beginning administrator will look quite different from one of a master administrator.

How to Use This Book

A glossary of terms is located at the end of the book to strengthen a common leadership language. Each chapter of this book is organized to guide the reader through several steps, culminating in the completion of a meaningful professional portfolio.

Step 1: Gaining insight into the theoretical basis of the standards
Step 2: Bridging theory into practice by connecting the standards to the everyday work of a school leader
Step 3: Developing and completing a portfolio entry (selecting and preparing artifacts, writing reflection narratives, and assembling the entry)
Step 4: Reviewing a sample portfolio entry to gain an understanding of the process
Step 5: Participating in an interactive exercise, giving the reader an opportunity to respond to a sample entry based on a case study and to make improvements to the entry

The CD-ROM included with this textbook includes additional resources available on the Internet, as well as a full treatment of each standard, including case studies, portfolio exercises, and self-assessment tools for student analysis and review.

Acknowledgments

We would like to thank the following colleagues for their contributions to this textbook and its accompanying CD-ROM materials: Robert Colon, Mary Didelot, Lisa Hollingsworth, Nadine Roush, and Anastasia Trekles. We would also like to thank the reviewers for this edition: Felicia Blacher-Wilson, Xavier University of Louisiana; John Daresh, University of Texas at El Paso; Suzanne Gilmour, SUNY Oswego; Margaret Grogan, University of Missouri-Columbia; Mary K. McCullough, Loyola Marymount University; Anthony Normore, Florida International University; Patricia Rea, George Washington University; James J. Rivard, Oakland University & Marygrove College; Nancy Schilling, Northern Arizona University; Nancy H. Stankus, Shippensburg University of Pennsylvania; and David E. Whale, Central Michigan University.

1 Standard 1: A Vision of Learning

The heart of leadership lives in the hearts of leaders.

—Bolman and Deal, 1995

A school administrator is an educational leader who promotes the success of all students by facilitating the development, articulation, implementation, and stewardship of a vision of learning that is shared and supported by the greater school community.

OBJECTIVES

The learner will

- Understand the theory behind Standard 1
- Learn the emerging theories of values-laden professional relationships that bring meaning to a milieu of accountability
- Reflect on what actions bring about a shared vision in a school community
- Explore opportunities to use the knowledges and dispositions of Standard 1 in the everyday practice of school leadership
- Practice completing a portfolio entry for Standard 1
- Interact with a sample case study to put into practice the details of a reflection narrative for a portfolio entry

Part 1: Examining Standard 1

A Changing View of Leadership

Prior to developing a portfolio based on the standard dealing with **leadership** and **vision**, it is important to understand the emerging leadership theories that serve as the standard's foundation. School leadership theory evolved during the 1970s and 1980s into what most educators referred to as the *instructional leadership model.* As a reaction to the prevailing theories of the 1940s through the 1970s that emphasized the importance of administrative management, theorists in the 1980s and 1990s attempted to explore leadership theory as one in which there was a lesser management focus, with greater emphasis on student learning. Several writers proposed elaborate models of effective leadership, and preparatory texts added tables showing steps to effective leadership based on scientific research into the most effective schools and their leaders' behaviors. Representative theories of prominence during the period between 1960 and 1980 are displayed in Table 1.1. These theories continue to influence leadership today.

Although these theories offer helpful insight into leadership styles, they must be complemented when placed in the current milieu of swirling change, public pressure for accountability, and teacher empowerment.

The Emergence of New Theory

Recent literature in school administration has emphasized the nebulous, chaotic, and unpredictable nature of leadership. Since the 1990s, theorists have emphasized that leadership cannot be charted, neatly described, nor prescripted. Writers such as Fullan, Senge, Sergiovanni, Bolman, Deal, and Heifetz write about the unstable nature of change and the high risk leaders assume in such an environment. Heifetz (1994) writes in *Leadership Without Easy Answers* that issues society faces require leadership that challenge us to confront "problems for which there are no simple, painless solutions . . . problems that require us to learn new ways to lead . . . . Making progress on these problems demands not just someone who provides answers from on high but changes our attitudes, behavior, and values" (p. 13). In other words, the prevailing theories of the 1970s and 1980s are now manifested in new theories of leadership. Writers during the '70s and '80s emphasized that effective leaders needed to follow certain prescribed steps to ensure success. During that same era, textbooks in leadership preparation programs "listed" various ways to become a successful leader, such as site-based management, developing a school **mission**, becoming an instructional leader, and so on. New challenges of the twenty-first century, however, demand innovation and discovery instead of ready-made answers. Peter Senge (1994), in *The Fifth*

TABLE 1.1   Summary of Representative Prominent Leadership Theories

Theory	Contention
Maslow's Needs Hierarchy	Effective leaders will recognize how psychological needs manifest themselves in human behavior and will thereby make appropriate decisions regarding staff impact. (McGregor, 1960).
Herzberg's Motivation—Hygiene Theory	Hygiene factors are part of the work environment. Motivating factors are part of workers' self-actualization and self-esteem. Effective leaders distinguish between these factors, making decisions based on them. (Herzberg, 1993).

Discipline, speaks of understanding the importance of looking inward before attempting to lead others. He writes,

> The discipline starts with turning the mirror inward; learning to unearth our internal pictures of the world, to bring them to the surface and hold them rigorously to scrutiny. It also includes the ability to carry on "learningful" conversations that balance inquiry and advocacy, where people expose their own thinking effectively and make that thinking open to the influence of others. (p. 44)

Senge (1994) continues his explanation of new leadership theory with the following:

> Our traditional views of leaders—as special people who set the direction, make the key decisions, and energize the troops—are deeply rooted in an individualistic and nonsystemic worldview. Especially in the West, leaders are heroes—great men (and occasionally women) who "rise to the fore" in times of crises . . . . The new view of leadership . . . centers on subtler and more important tasks. In a learning organization, leaders are designers, stewards, and teachers. They are responsible for building organizations where people continually expand their capabilities to understand complexity, clarify vision, and improve shared mental models—that is, they are responsible for learning. (p. 45)

Emergent leadership theory also addresses the unique needs of urban leadership and other issues-oriented contexts. Larson and Ovando (2001) argue that challenges in urban schools differ sharply from those of more affluent districts. They also point out that urban educators, especially minority women, view their communities as crucial to school success. For example, Murtadha Watts and Larson (1999) studied black female school leaders and found several key qualities that were common to their leadership. They listed the following as common characteristics of urban minority female leaders:

- A rational resistance to systems that failed to serve their families
- A reliance on black churches—the only truly African-American institution
- An understanding of the parental distrust and resistance to schools
- A sense of their lives as more than administrators, but rather mediators, mothers, ministers, neighbors, and counselors (as cited in Larson and Ovando, 2001, pp. 192–193)

Furthermore, when considering the issue of gender regarding leadership, writers such as Shakeshaft (1989) have shown that female school leaders have unique characteristics and styles, such as openness to curricular and pedagogical issues, a democratic style rather than autocratic, and a tendency to emphasize relationships over roles. Cordeiro (1999) further contends that Latino-Americans have unique leadership styles as well. These new issues-oriented theories are critical to the emerging literature on school leadership.

Relationships and Values

The emergent theories of leadership focus on the human side of schools and the importance of establishing relationships that are conducive to shared learning. The new administrator must "learn to learn," rather than attempt to "take charge" or "set the tone" for the school or district. Effective leaders must find a way to resonate with and embrace their constituencies. In other words, they must strike a chord of understanding and connection with all the **stakeholders** in the **school community**. Sergiovanni (1992) explains the importance of a values orientation in his book *Moral Leadership:* "We need to be in touch with our basic values and with our connections to others. In other words, we must become more authentic with ourselves and others. If we are successful, we will be able to transform schools from ordinary organizations into learning communities" (p. 29). In Table 1.2, the theorists emphasizing the human side of leadership are listed along with their most important ideas.

In summary, the new leadership theorists argue for the importance of

- Human relationships
- Emotional intelligence
- Inward reflection
- Following
- A values orientation

TABLE 1.2   Important Ideas from a Relationship and Values Orientation

Authors	Summary
Thomas Sergiovanni	The successful leader is one who builds up the leadership of others and who strives to become a leader of leaders. A successful leader is also a good follower—one who follows ideas, values, and beliefs. A new kind of hierarchy emerges in the school, one that places purposes, values, and commitments at the apex and teachers, principals, parents, and students below in service to these purposes (Sergiovanni, 2001, p. 150).
Robert Evans	Evans (1996) suggests, for example, that when veteran teachers are asked to embrace reforms, their psyche is telling them that they are experiencing loss and thus grief. They will often exhibit behaviors similar to those of people grieving over the loss of a loved one.
Ron Heifetz	When we look to authorities for answers to adaptive challenges, we end up with dysfunction (Heifetz, 1994, p. 18).
Michael Fullan	Realizing that there is no answer, that we will never arrive in any formal sense, can be quite liberating . . . . Leaders for change get involved as learners in real reform situations (Fullan, 1998, pp. 55–56).
Reginald Green	Leadership involves establishing relationships with people affiliated with the organization sufficient to gain their commitment (Green, 2001).
Lee Bolman and Terrence Deal	Spiritual concerns of the modern manager (Bolman & Deal, 1995, p. 12)
Paula Cordeiro	Total quality education (TQE) with multicultural teaching in positive and supporting ways (Cordeiro et al., 1994, Cordeiro, 1999)

- Designing
- Stewarding
- Teaching and learning
- Multicultural understanding

The following is an examination of how successful leaders can use the preceding ideas to bring educational stakeholders together in the quest toward a productive learning community. As discussed in the previous section, current theory suggests that effective leaders can lead with relationships and a values-laden orientation, even though the political climate suggests that school leaders should focus on results only, disregarding the needs of the human beings in the school community.

Part 2: Key Performances, Knowledges, and Dispositions for Standard 1

Key Performances

When considering emergent theories of leadership, an emphasis must be placed on the human side of change, the importance of emotional intelligence, and teaching and learning needs related to individual relationships and a values-laden orientation. At first glance, it would appear that these theories come into conflict with the prevailing political milieu of accountability, standardized tests, and "back to basics" paradigms. Perhaps the two competing concepts can exist peacefully together. If school leaders are going to be effective, they must accept the reality of a political climate underscored by data-driven accountability. Such an acceptance, however, does not necessarily mean that the leader must forego emphasis on human relationships. This book proposes that the best leadership pedagogy is one that accepts and embraces the reality of the current political climate while finding the means to build the capacity for sound, professional relationships laden with values. Effective school leaders must begin by forming a keen understanding of their own worldview. This can only be accomplished through serious reflection about what creates the leaders' responses, thoughts, and actions—a strong values orientation. Second, effective leaders will "learn to learn" by opening their minds and hearts to the worldviews of those with whom they work in the **school community**. Third, effective leaders will develop their emotional intelligence and garner expertise in forming professional, productive, and satisfying relationships with their colleagues. Lastly, effective leaders will learn to design and to steward their communities toward positive change and productive learning centers.

The next section of this chapter will examine how a shared vision can be crafted using performances from the first standard developed by the ISLLC (2000). Each of the succeeding performances will be discussed with suggestions for developing these elements in administrative practice.

Performances
1. Core beliefs of the school are modeled for all **stakeholders**
2. The vision is developed with and among stakeholders

3. The vision shapes the educational programs, plans, and actions
4. An implementation plan is developed in which objectives and strategies to achieve the vision and goals are clearly articulated
5. The vision, mission, and implementation plans are regularly monitored, evaluated, and revised

Modeling Core Beliefs

Effective school leaders must look inward at their own beliefs before assuming a key role in vision development and visioning with all members of the school community. To model and acculturate core beliefs, wise school leaders must take a serious look at what they value as core beliefs. The following questions must be answered honestly at the outset:

- Do I really believe that *all* children can learn?
- As an educational leader, how do I promote a belief in the potential for *all* children to learn? What actions or evidence demonstrate such a belief?
- What personal and professional experiences helped me reach this belief?
- What do I believe are appropriate steps when a child does not seem to be learning even after a myriad of strategies have been exhausted? What capacities have I created or should create?

Effective leaders will reflect carefully on their answers to these questions. In addition, they will encourage their staff to do the same. An honest appraisal of the community's core belief in the success of *all* students should follow. The leader and the larger community must develop a plan to ensure that the group's beliefs are implemented in the everyday activities of the school community. In addition, the school leader must take every opportunity to model the core beliefs in a sincere and authentic fashion. If a leader makes a concerted effort to model the core beliefs of the school and the community, then the proper performances will follow. This will take practice and patience, but it can be accomplished.

Developing the Shared Vision of Learning

Phase 1: Development of the Vision.   Once leaders thoughtfully reflect on their core beliefs regarding the learning potential of *all* children, they can begin to facilitate the development, articulation, stewardship, and implementation of a vision of learning. Senge, Sergiovanni, Fullan, and Heifetz are the most prominent theorists of recent literature concerning vision development. They all stress the importance of a leader's willingness to listen, learn, and follow, rather than a tendency to lead, direct, and dominate. Before school leaders can hope to move a diverse base of educational stakeholders toward consensus on a shared vision, they must learn to be learners. This entails the ability truly to hear what other stakeholders, both internal and external to the school or district, are saying. Effective leaders will spend sufficient time listening thoughtfully to all stakeholders, then reflecting quietly about the values and meaning behind the words. Stakeholders often communicate a much deeper meaning than their written or spoken words—something well understood by leaders who not only "hear," but "listen." Effective leaders will learn to clarify what stakeholders are saying by using questioning techniques such as, "If I understand you correctly . . ." or "I would like to summarize what has been said . . ." Most important, though, leaders must sincerely want to understand. No amount of strategizing will cover up a leader's lack of sincerity or empathy.

Fullan (1998) suggests that good leaders must also learn to welcome conflict and allow it to occur. He maintains that vision building must include a certain amount of conflict and tension. Effective leaders will allow plenty of time for stakeholders to wrestle with their differences, creating capacities for these differences to be valued among all stakeholders. In addition, effective leaders will invite informed differences as a part of **consensus** building and **collaboration**. These same leaders have realistic expectations that groups will struggle with their attempts to build a vision. Ineffective leaders will expect the process to follow a neat and tidy pattern, moving seamlessly through prescribed steps. Vision building takes time and patience.

Phase 2: Articulation of the Vision into the School Programs. Once the thorough process of developing a shared vision is complete, the leader can begin to facilitate the articulation, stewardship, and implementation of the vision. Articulating the vision entails infusing the vision into all aspects of the school experience—from classrooms to newsletters, from sports events to buses. Effective leaders will invite all stakeholders to suggest means that ensure the vision is embedded in all aspects of the school or district. During this phase, effective leaders will support the leadership of others by empowerment with a high degree of trust. Nothing will increase stakeholder efficacy faster than empowerment in a values-infused environment. Literature findings on school leadership emphasize a concept called *distributed leadership.* In other words, informed building and district leaders understand the effectiveness of sharing leadership with empowered and entrusted staff members. Killion (2005) suggests that "the complex tasks of a school leader must be distributed or shared." A wise leader will allow two or more teachers and parents to form a committee charged with planning capacities for the vision to permeate the school experience. The leader must thoughtfully facilitate a sustained focus on the key elements of strategic planning to ensure the initiative's success. In other words, the leader should demonstrate to the staff how to form a plan of action using steps such as (1) establishing a baseline of evidence, (2) participating in activities for each step along the way, (3) articulating stakeholder responsibilities, and (4) assessing evidence through measured outcomes.

Phase 3: Monitoring the Vision. Stewardship of the vision implies an assurance that the vision is nurtured and monitored. Initially the vision is fresh and the school community happily embraces it, but soon the interest will invariably wane. Effective leaders will recognize the natural tendency of people to tire quickly and to want to move on to new challenges, especially if the vision is not embedded in the culture. Whether considering the vision at the building level or district level, untended, quickly contrived, or banal vision statements that lack meaning are often the brunt of professional jokes, lost in the plethora of policy and governance initiatives. Effective leaders encourage stakeholders to focus on teaching and learning that keeps the vision vibrant and meaningful. Committees or advisories are often excellent venues, when charged with vision/mission accomplishment, to find ways of keeping the vision from becoming stale and meaningless. The committee or advisory could make regular reports at staff meetings, allowing everyone to react to their information. Group roles and expectations should be carefully articulated, with particular attention given to the evidence and outcomes that will inform the group's work. The committee or advisory might begin an ongoing check of how the vision is being realized at the classroom level. Teachers could share how they have used the vision to inform and enhance teaching and learning, for example.

Phase 4: Implementation: Data Analysis.   The implementation phase is cause for celebration and is also a source challenge—a learning environment in which the vision is continuously demonstrated. It is one thing to develop and articulate a vision, but it is quite another to infuse the vision in the daily work of the building or district. Implementation will require regular opportunities to discuss and share how the vision is being demonstrated. Effective leaders will assist their stakeholders in gathering data to evidence whether the vision is being implemented. Then they can demonstrate how the data can be interpreted to determine what is working and what is not.

Remember the Human Side of Leadership

Developing a shared vision of learning will be marginalized if capacities do not exist within the organization's culture that are defined by trust, motivation, collaboration, and celebration. Educational stakeholders need an environment that is supportive and rewarding. Effective leaders will regularly find ways to express genuine thanks and to recognize their stakeholders, to support their work, and to celebrate their successes with them. This is done one-to-one, in small and large groups (e.g., special dinners or luncheons), and with the use of one-way communiqués (e.g., e-mail or note). Investing in interpersonal skills to define leadership can accomplish amazing things for teaching and learning. Leaders who display effective "people skills" (i.e., interpersonal skills) will find themselves surrounded by dedicated stakeholders who are motivated to reach their full potential amidst the complex tasks of teaching and learning.

Representative Comments Demonstrating Emerging Performances for Standard 1

- "We are proud that the school's mission reflects the consensus of faculty, staff, students, parents, and community members. You'll find it displayed in all our newsletters and correspondence."
- "We believe all our students can learn. In what ways can we better address the learning needs of your child?"
- "Okay. If we say that all children can learn, how are we demonstrating this in the classrooms? Let's spend some time today in small groups talking about this."
- "Now that we have developed a vision and mission, let's define a plan of action to accomplish the mission and arrive at the vision. Let's consider how everyone can support the plan of action."

Representative Actions Demonstrating Emerging Performances for Standard 1

- The principal provides a copy of the school mission/vision for all faculty and staff to display throughout the school. Teachers are later asked how teaching and learning are supportive of the mission/vision.
- The school newsletter and other one-way communiqués always prominently display the mission/vision.
- Staff meetings always begin with a discussion of the mission/vision, and a plan is supported that ensures the mission/vision is being implemented.
- The principal takes advantage of opportunities in a bus driver's meeting to speak about the mission/vision and to model practices that are supportive of the powerful statements.
- The principal forms a parent and community advisory council to strengthen school–community relations. Their work is grounded in the mission/vision.
- The superintendent ensures there is alignment between the district's mission/vision and those of the buildings.

Key Knowledges and Dispositions

Previously, this chapter has demonstrated how an effective administrator will use the performances associated with Standard 1 to develop a shared vision of learning. In addition to performances, Standard 1 contains knowledges and dispositions. This section will assist the administrator in building behaviors that demonstrate attainment of the knowledges and dispositions. The following list details those key knowledges and dispositions from Standard 1:

Knowledges
The administrator has a knowledge and understanding of

1. Learning goals in a pluralistic society
2. The principles of developing and implementing strategic plans
3. Theories of educational leadership (e.g., the categories of systems theory, change theory, and motivational theory)
4. Information sources, data collection, and data analysis strategies
5. Effective communication (e.g., writing, speaking, listening, use of technology)
6. Negotiation skills for consensus building
7. The foundations of education

Dispositions
The administrator believes in, values, and is committed to

1. The educability of all
2. The ideal of the common good
3. A school vision of high standards of learning
4. Inclusion of all stakeholders

It is clear that the knowledges and dispositions for Standard 1 are closely aligned with the concepts presented earlier in this section. When combined, an effective leader understands how to build consensus, how to manage data, how to communicate effectively, and has a keen understanding of leadership theory. Second, an effective leader holds firm beliefs about the educability of all, the importance of high expectations, and the necessity of focusing on the common good. These understandings and attitudes are demonstrated in the actions and the words of the leader.

Key Knowledges

The knowledges are broad and have a great deal of depth and meaning for school leaders. First, the leader must understand how the multiple variations in modern culture influence a school setting. Political and legal trends impact the school setting in various ways. For example, curriculum development in the United States has changed drastically during the past 50 years as ever-growing recognition is given to subcultures and alternative life styles. A modern school leader must ensure that everyone in the school community is valued. In other words, an effective leader values **diversity** in the broadest sense.

Second, an effective leader must embrace strategic planning principles. Decision making must be based on a consistent pedagogy that is based on baseline data, goals and objectives, time lines, personnel assignments, and measurable outcomes. Third, an effective leader understands the theories behind leadership and the foundations of education. As previously discussed, the new theories of leadership emphasize the chaotic, unpredictable, and emotional-laden aspects of school change. A wise leader uses theory to form a well-developed pedagogy of leadership and learning-centered issues.

Fourth, an effective leader understands the importance of good communication. This means establishing multiple communication venues with school–community stakeholders on a sustained basis. The effective leader also invests in communication as a means of developing capacities for consensus and strengthening professional relationships. This takes practice, but is an essential skill that must be developed. Genuine consensus does not have "losers" or "winners." Rather, all stakeholders believe they had meaningful input into decision making, underscored in a climate of cooperation and value for diversity of opinion.

The following lists give representative examples of how leaders can demonstrate these key knowledges by comments and by actions:

Representative Comments Demonstrating Emerging Knowledges for Standard 1

- "I noticed that you continually encourage your students by words and actions that communicate you believe in them. Your commitment to help them succeed is genuinely appreciated."
- "I hope you'll consider becoming an administrator some day. Your teacher–leadership efforts have improved teaching and learning in the district."
- "We've discussed many challenges and I agree that they must be addressed; however, for the purposes of this community advisory committee, let's revisit our original charge to guide our work."
- "Whenever I walk through this school, I always see displays of students' work, indicative of a learner-centered environment."

Representative Actions Demonstrating Emerging Knowledges for Standard 1

- The leader reaches to a larger school community by using newsletters, memos, and personal notes to clarify and articulate the importance of shared vision, often relying on examples in practice.
- The administrator keeps a journal of self-reflection addressing personal changes in views of leadership.
- The leader seeks resources from the community and other external sources to improve teaching and learning.
- The budget is evaluated in light of the vision, mission, and assessment systems.

Key Dispositions

Effective leaders must have well-articulated attitudes and beliefs about schooling. First, they must believe that *all* children can learn. This is best evidenced through the leader's actions and words. Second, they must promote the ideal of the common good. To focus on the common good minimizes a "me first" orientation. Third, effective leaders hold high expectations for *all* learners. High expectations move beyond minimums, acknowledging the diversity of learners and the potential they might achieve. Fourth, effective leaders reach out to *all* members of the school community. These leaders value and embrace a broad landscape of educational stakeholders to inform and enhance the school's and district's efforts.

The following lists contain representative dispositional samples of comments and actions that effective leaders demonstrate for Standard 1.

Representative Comments Demonstrating Emerging Dispositions for Standard 1

- "The decision was difficult, but represented the consensus of the district's improvement committee. Many solutions were considered and the final decision best represents the interests of the entire district."
- "Thank you for sharing your perspective. I understand your urgency in wanting a decision, but in all fairness to the others involved, I'll need more time to look into this with greater depth. I can assure you this issue will be addressed immediately."
- "An invitation was mailed last week, but I wanted to invite you personally to our advisory meeting. Your perspective would be greatly valued."
- "In the past, I've allocated a per-student dollar amount to schools for capital expenditures. In the future, I'll be considering 'adequacy' needs. How might we define the adequate resource expenditure?"

Representative Actions Demonstrating Emerging Dispositions for Standard 1

- The leader sets clear expectations for students and staff, and celebrates their attainment of those expectations.
- The leader is heard making comments to staff and students that show a firm belief in the educability of all.
- The leader spends extra hours with parents or students, assisting them with academic challenges.
- The leader advocates for academic programs that values learners of all exceptionalities.

The previous analysis is only a brief overview of how the standard can take on meaning in the administrator's day. Specific steps for building the portfolio are discussed in the next section. In addition, refer to the accompanying CD-ROM for further activities related to Standard 1.

Part 3: Portfolio Exercise for Standard 1

The following exercise will help students seeking administrative licensure to build their professional portfolios. Procedures are described here that will lead to a completed entry for a professional portfolio (Standard 1: A Vision of Learning). A five-level scoring rubric to measure the level of standard attainment is contained in Appendix B. The rubric provides the rater with scoring criteria to evaluate the portfolio exercise.

Initial Setup of the Portfolio Box

1. Obtain a file box for storing file folders.
2. Place six or eight (six for building level and eight for district level) dividers in the box and label them Standard 1, Standard 2, and so forth.
3. Place three manila folders in each divider.

First Exercise

1. Access your file box and find the divider for Standard 1.
2. Consider the phases of creating a shared vision and the key performances discussed in Chapter 1. Think about in which activities a leader would be engaged to demonstrate these phases. Choose one activity that you will develop in your school setting. Examples include setting up a staff meeting to discuss a shared vision; creating examples of vision articulation such as posters, newsletter, and logos; or convening an advisory committee to address challenging school–community issues, such as parent involvement. Think about the knowledges and dispositions associated with Standard 1 and discuss them in your narrative section.
3. Conduct the activity and keep a record using a video or audio recorder.
4. Review the video/audio recording and write a reflection about what happened. The reflection should include a description of the setting (place, time, participants, etc.), what happened and why (analysis), and what you found was successful as well as what you would do differently if you had the opportunity (reflection).
5. Write about how the activity demonstrates your attainment of the standard.
6. Provide written authenticity for the activity. For example, your supervisor writes a letter attesting to your performance of the activity, or a policy statement is developed and shared.
7. Place the video- or audiotape in the divider for Standard 1. Place the written samples in the folders.
8. Carefully review all items and correct any errors.

A sample cover sheet and reflection narrative follow.

BOX **1.1**

Sample Portfolio Entry

Artifact for Standard 1: A Vision of Learning

Name of Artifact: Workshop on Integrating Technology

Date: October 10, 20XX

Johnston School District, Johnston City, OK

Artifact

I have included a video of the workshop. The video contains 30 minutes of unedited coverage of the workshop. I opened the meeting by introducing our guests and discussing the vision again for our school. Next, I distributed and discussed the student learning standards. Finally, I facilitated the work of participants in small groups.

Reflection Narrative

In mid October I presented a half-day workshop to the staff of three schools in our district about effectively integrating technology into the curriculum. This was the third in a series of workshops on this subject. Last year, the district's school improvement team identified this as a need and established it as one of the goals in our improvement plan. The district team had previously identified integrating technology as a key in reaching our vision of "Every Student Learning." At the request of the team, I surveyed district staff to learn more about their needs for professional development in this area. After examining their responses, I noted that most felt a need for additional training in integrating technology with language instruction. This is not my area of expertise, so I sought the input of staff and administrators, researching a variety of available software programs. I then arranged staff training for the two programs that I felt would best meet their needs. Two other principals outside my district expressed an interest in the same topic, so I invited them to send staff members to this workshop. To begin the workshop, I distributed copies of the state student learning standards to every teacher present. They worked in small groups to identify the standards that they thought could be taught using technology. Next, we moved to the computer lab, where I introduced the staff to two new programs that could enhance the teaching of language standards. One program involves students in proofreading edited written copy for errors in grammar, punctuation, and spelling. The other allows students to create graphic organizers to share information or to plan for writing. After watching a demonstration of the two programs, teachers had an opportunity to try them. To conclude the afternoon, each teacher was asked to discuss a grade-level standard and tell how he or she would use the new programs to meet the standard.

Staff response to the workshop and the new programs was positive. On the workshop evaluation forms, 82% of the participants rated the workshop as "very helpful," 14% rated it "somewhat helpful," and 4% rated it "not helpful." Almost all the teachers present were able to identify specific standards they could teach using the new programs. One staff member showed resistance to implementing the new programs. He was doubtful that the programs would be useful because the lab is rarely available and the equipment is often broken. This may be an indication that he is fearful of the new technology. The visiting staff outside the district seemed receptive to the training.

In the weeks since this workshop took place, I have observed teachers using the new technology to help students meet the standards. I would like to plan a follow-up workshop to allow teachers to share ways they are using the new programs in their classrooms and to do grade-level planning of specific strategies for integrating these new programs into their curriculum. I plan to

(continued)

BOX **1.1**   **Continued**

initiate cross-grade-level classroom partnering with some classes. This will provide teachers with peer-to-peer mentoring opportunities. My hope is that by continuing to monitor the program's implementation, I can confidently say that our vision is being implemented in the classroom.

Scoring Analysis for the Entry
Using the portfolio exercise scoring rubric (see Appendix B), this entry would score a 5. There is clear and compelling evidence of the principal's consistent work to improve the school and to advance the vision to the staff within that school. The description sets the context and background that show how this is part of an ongoing program to meet specifically identified school improvement goals. The analysis of the response of the workshop's target audience is somewhat superficial, but a potential problem is identified (i.e., resistance on the part of a staff member) and is addressed in the reflection part of the narrative. A specific strategy is suggested for addressing the problem (cross-grade-level classroom partnering). A specific goal is given for the next workshop, which is clearly related to the preceding workshops. The administrator has provided clear evidence of attainment of Standard 1 in the manner in which the workshop was planned, implemented, and evaluated. Had the administrator failed to provide evidence of efforts toward vision alignment, the score would have been much lower.

Suggestions for Standard 1 Sample Artifacts
- Video of candidate conducting a staff meeting in which the vision is discussed
- A collection of newsletters and memos showing a plan for setting the vision
- Audiotape of candidate speaking with parents about the school's vision
- A report to the superintendent about the school community's plan for a shared vision
- A report to the school board explaining the superintendent's conception of a shared vision for the district

Part 4: Case Study, Standard 1

Read the scenario that follows and answer the questions provided at the end. Sample answers to each question are provided on the enclosed CD-ROM to guide you.

Sally Jones is a first-year principal at Beech Grove Middle School. She is following a popular principal who retired after 30 years at the same school. The staff had grown accustomed to their former principal, and a culture had developed that allowed for some rituals that Sally wants to address. For example, on Friday afternoons students could watch videos or cable broadcasts while the teachers "caught up." Change was not being embraced and an attitude of "status quo" permeated the building. A shared school vision was completely out of the question unless Sally could pull a rabbit out of her hat and convince the staff that changes were needed. As she contemplates her portfolio entry for Standard 1, she wonders how she will begin to facilitate a shared vision that is truly student focused. She decides to embark on a plan to change the instructional climate in the sixth grades. First, she requests a meeting with the sixth grade team. She tells them that she is interested in finding out more about "**best practices**" with regard to transitions (i.e., fifth to sixth grade). She has a friend at the nearby university who works in educational programming. One of her assignments includes the creation of "learning communities" in classrooms. Sally asks the sixth-grade team to take a "leap of faith" with her to find out more about learning communities. Promising to find grant funds, Sally asks if they would be interested in attending a state meeting about the program. Two of the teachers respond immediately with enthusiasm, but the other five are less than enthusiastic. Sally suggests that the two interested teachers attend the meeting with her and report back. Everyone agrees with the idea, and Sally happily makes arrangements for the teachers to accompany her to the state capital for the meeting. In the meantime, two of the remaining five teachers decide that they would like to go along as well. Sally is ecstatic; she now has four teachers willing to take a professional journey with her! She decides that following the meeting at the state capital she will ask the attendees to report back what they learned to the other three teachers who did not attend. During that meeting she hopes that together they can brainstorm a plan of action to initiate the program in a small way as a one-year pilot. Sally decides to videotape the meeting and use it as an artifact for her Standard 1 entry.

> *Question 1:* Do you think that Sally's idea to use the meeting as an artifact for Standard 1 is appropriate? Why or why not?
>
> *Question 2:* Imagine that you are Sally. Write a reflection narrative about the meeting, using your imagination as to what occurs. Remember to include a description of the setting, participants, and purpose of the meeting. Second, write an analysis of what happened. Third, write your reflection about what you think happened that showed attainment or lack thereof of Standard 1. What performances, knowledges, and dispositions did you show during the meeting? Did you accomplish what you had hoped? Would you do something differently if you had the chance?
>
> *Question 3:* If you were Sally, would you have taken the same first steps to initiate a learning community initiative? What would you have done differently? What other artifacts would you have used to show attainment of Standard 1?

2 Standard 2: School Culture and Instructional Program

A school's culture is always at work, either helping or hindering . . . learning.

—Peterson, 2002, p. 1

A school administrator is an educational leader who promotes the success of all students and staff by advocating, nurturing, and sustaining a school culture and instructional program conducive to student learning and staff professional growth.

OBJECTIVES

The learner will

■ Understand the research relating to instructional program and **school culture**

■ Understand how to create an effective instructional program

■ Learn how to create a healthy school culture

■ Explore ways to put the knowledges and dispositions from Standard 2 into everyday practice

■ Practice completing an entry for Standard 2

■ Develop an understanding of a reflection narrative

Part 1: Examining Standard 2

Leadership and School Culture

If school leaders are to accomplish the conceptions of Standard 2, they must understand what is meant by *advocating, nurturing, and sustaining a school culture and instructional program conducive to student learning and staff professional growth.* To come to this understanding, it is first important to look at what prominent theorists are saying about school culture and the instructional program.

Defining School Culture

Deal and Peterson (1999) define school culture as the "set of norms, values and beliefs, rituals and ceremonies, symbols and stories that make up the 'persona' of the school" (pp. 22–23). They add,

Schools have rituals and ceremonies—communal events to celebrate success, to provide closure during collective transitions, and to recognize people's contributions to the school. School cultures also include symbols and stories that communicate core values, reinforce the mission, and build a shared sense of commitment. (as cited in Peterson, 2002, p. 1)

During the 1990s, educational researchers and theorists began to use the term *culture* in addition to the traditional term *climate*. When writers describe **school climate,** they most often refer to a safe and orderly environment. The concept of a school's climate, however, is no longer broad enough to explain the breadth and depth of an entire school community's interactions and experiences over time. Although safety and order are certainly important to a school's success, they can be subsumed under the broader term of *culture*. Sergiovanni (1984) describes culture as "the collective programming of the mind that distinguishes the members of one school from another" (p. 32). Leaders play an important role in creating a school culture that includes values, symbols, beliefs, and shared meanings for parents. A school's culture is evident within the first few moments of entering the school. The school's traditions and shared understandings collectively make up the personality or essence of a school (Sergiovanni, 1984).

Schein (1984) contends that the strength of a culture can be affected by the length and consistency of the group's experiences. If a staff has had a long, varied, and intense history, it will have a strong and diverse culture. If there is a lot of shifting and turnover in staff, the culture will be weaker. However, a culture can survive a high turnover rate if the leadership remains stable (Schein, 1984).

Writers such as Peterson, Deal, and DuFour have described the importance of a healthy culture in schools. Peterson (2002) writes:

Every organization has a culture, that history and underlying set of unwritten expectations that shape everything about the school. A school culture influences the ways people think, feel, and act. Being able to understand and shape the culture is key to a school's success in promoting staff and student learning. (p. 22)

Healthy Versus Toxic Cultures

Stein, Fullan, and DuFour, among others, have all suggested that cultures in schools are either positive or negative. They contend that effective school leaders ensure that the following traits are found in healthy school cultures:

- A widely shared sense of purpose and values
- Norms of continuous learning and improvement
- A commitment to and sense of responsibility for the learning of all students
- Collaborative, collegial relationships
- Opportunities for staff reflection, collective inquiry, and sharing personal practice (DuFour & Eaker, 1998; Fullan, 2001; Hord, 1998; Lambert, 1998; Stein, 1998)

Additionally, these schools often have a common professional language, shared stories of success, multiple opportunities for quality professional development, and ceremonies that celebrate improvement, collaboration, and learning (Peterson & Deal, 2002). When school leaders can bring about school characteristics such as these, then they are in fact creating a *school culture and instructional program conducive to student learning and staff professional growth* (ISLLC, 2000, Standard 2).

On the other hand, some schools have negative cultures with "toxic" norms and values that work against growth and learning. As Peterson (2002) contends, "schools with toxic cultures lack a clear sense of purpose, have norms that reinforce inertia, blame students for lack of progress, discourage collaboration, and often have actively hostile relations among staff. These schools are not healthy for staff or students" (p. 31).

Leaders are the key to determining whether a school community has a healthy or a toxic culture. Effective leaders will work with their staff and communities to ensure that the school's culture includes high-quality staff development, ceremonies and celebrations, and collaboration. Peterson and Deal (2002) suggest that school leaders create healthy cultures through several key processes:

- Read the culture, understanding the culture's historical source as well as analyzing current norms and values.
- Assess the culture, determining which elements of the culture support the school's core purposes and the mission, and which hinder achieving valued ends.
- Actively shape the culture by reinforcing positive aspects and by working to transform negative aspects of the culture. (p. 54)

DuFour (2003) also emphasizes the leader's role in creating a healthy culture. He contends that leaders are asking the wrong questions as they try to be effective "instructional leaders." DuFour suggests that instead of asking, *What are the teachers teaching?* and *How can I help them to teach it more effectively?* they should ask, *To what extent are the students learning the intended outcomes of each course?* and *What steps can I take to give both students and teachers the additional time and support they need to improve learning?* (pp. 36–37).

Determining Whether a Culture Is Healthy or Toxic

Effective leaders create a healthy school culture by creating a vision and common mission, teaching and coaching teachers, encouraging risk taking, and developing trust and respect. A school culture either sabotages quality professional learning or supports authentic professional development. A wise school leader will learn how to develop and sustain a positive, professional culture that nurtures staff learning. In addition, a wise leader will know that keeping a healthy culture is the task of everyone in the school. With a strong, positive culture that supports professional development and student learning, schools can become places where every teacher feels respected and every child learns.

Peterson and Deal (2002) suggest that principals can evaluate the culture of the school by talking to the school's staff, many of whom have been around several years and enjoy talking about the school's history. In addition, leaders can study school improvement plans by looking for indications about what is most important, or they can use a staff meeting to discuss what has occurred in staff development in the past. They write,

> It is important to examine contemporary aspects of the culture. For example, asking each staff member to list six adjectives to describe the school, asking staff to tell a story that char-

acterizes what the school is about, or having staff write metaphors describing the school can reveal aspects of the school culture. (p. 3)

Peterson and Deal (2002) note that two important questions should be answered following the culture assessment steps:

1. What aspects of the culture are positive and should be reinforced?
2. What aspects of the culture are negative and harmful, and should be changed? (p. 4)

Another effective tool to assess the culture is a school culture survey (Richardson, 2001). Leaders can collect the survey results to see how strongly held different norms or values are, then determine whether they fit the culture the school is seeking to create. Peterson and Deal (2002) conclude with these statements:

> Leaders . . . can reinforce norms and values in their daily work, their words, and their interactions. They can establish rituals and traditions that make staff development an opportunity for culture building as well as learning. Staff and administrators may also need to change negative and harmful aspects of the culture. This is not easy. It is done by addressing the negative directly, finding examples of success to counteract stories of failure, impeding those who try to sabotage or criticize staff learning, and replacing negative stories of professional development with concrete positive results. (p. 5)

Leadership and the Instructional Program

The second part of Standard 2 refers to the instructional program. Only recently have researchers begun to show that the building and district leaders are key components in a successful instructional program. Many theorists are showing a clear connection between school leaders and student learning. Their research shows that strong leadership

- Creates the educational direction (McKay, 1999)
- Sets the tone for educational quality (Hopkins, 2002)
- Ensures each child reaches not only his/her academic potential, but his/her human potential (Pasi, 2001)
- Establishes a climate of physical and emotional safety combined with cognitive challenges (Pasi, 2001)
- Raises student achievement (Harris, 2001)
- Models the value of teaching and learning (Marriott, 2001)
- Encourage rigorous content within the classroom (Cooney, Moore, & Bottoms, 2002)
- Acts through powerful policy decisions and implementations (Marriott, 2001)

It is the school leader, then, who creates the capacity within higher performing schools to move students and teachers toward their individual potentials through a rigorous and demanding curriculum within a safe, supportive environment (Cooney, Moore, & Bottoms, 2002). Yet, responses are ambivalent when citizens are asked, Who or what is the essential ingredient in school success? It is rare that anyone identifies school leadership (Harris, 2001). Teachers, however, know better.

The Role of the Leader in the Instructional Program

Literature concerning the school leader's ability to bring about improved student achievement is profoundly clear. Educators know that leadership is central to the intricate weave of dynamic, complex relationships within a building and district. For teachers, a school leader must demonstrate a professional expertise with a moral imperative (Clarke, 2000). How do educators see this expertise and imperative implemented within a school district? Educators know that an effective leader is one who is

- A cooperative and communicative decision maker about learning (Clarke, 2000)
- A leader in learning (Davis, 2001)
- An analyzer who uses collaboration as a tool in his/her own learning (Davis, 2001)
- A purger of ineffective teachers (Davis, 2001)
- A supporter of individual teacher's pedagogy (Davis, 2001)
- A visible figure in classrooms for teacher professional improvement (Johnson, Kardos, Birkeland, et al., 2001)
- A provider of feedback for teachers' pedagogy (Johnson, Kardos, Birkeland, et al., 2001)
- A facilitator in problem resolution (Beerman & Kowalski, 1998)

For effective schools and districts, then, educators not only recognize the absolute need for strong leadership, but also fully welcome it. It is the school leader who allows educators to maximize each and every teaching opportunity (Chute, 1999).

It is not only teachers who want leaders who give focused attention to the acts of learning and teaching; wise school leaders want to do this as well. Effective school leaders know the way to improve student performance is to immerse themselves in the process of teaching and learning (EdSource, 1998). Building and district leaders welcome opportunities to engage in instructional/curriculum issue and planning, evaluation, and reform. They understand this is a competing demand with time spent on a multitude of management tasks, yet they know this is how to improve the quality of teaching and learning.

Creating a Strong Instructional Program

Glickman (1991) defines the primary tasks of instructional leadership as

- Direct assistance to teachers
- Group development
- Staff development
- Curriculum development
- Action research (p. 7)

He also notes that when leaders can integrate these tasks, it creates a positive impact on the culture of a school by uniting the teachers' needs with common school goals (Glickman, 1991).

Seyfarth and Nowinski (1987), like Glickman, cite direct assistance as a key element for administrators to improve classroom instruction and, ultimately, student achievement by focusing on improving school culture. Their research indicated that administrators must provide an environment in which teachers receive frequent feedback about their practices.

They interviewed 71 teachers to learn about their opinions of peer observers and about evaluation in general. Their findings revealed

- Teachers received relatively little feedback about their performance from principals
- Teachers preferred administrator evaluators to teacher evaluators
- Peer feedback was often unplanned and sporadic
- Teachers relied on the task environment for feedback (Seyfarth & Nowinski, 1987, pp. 48–49)

Creating an environment in which teachers feel free to take risks and thereby to improve their instruction is a daunting task for a school leader. A first step is to let teachers share important information about what works in their classrooms. As building leaders work to restructure their roles to include more teacher-centered feedback, they must consider the scope of such a shift. Creating a culture for change is often riddled with challenges that can be overwhelming for school administrators. To avoid the frustrations and pitfalls that are typically present during organizational change, Fullan (1991) offers 10 guidelines to help overcome the system inertia by placing the responsibility for initiation on the individual:

1. Avoid "if only" statements, externalizing the blame, and other forms of wishful thinking.
2. Start small; think big. Don't overplan or overmanage.
3. Focus on something concrete and important, like curriculum and instruction.
4. Focus on something fundamental, like the professional culture of the school.
5. Practice fearlessness and other forms of risk taking.
6. Empower others below you.
7. Build a vision in relation to both goals and change processes.
8. Decide what you are *not* going to do.
9. Build allies.
10. Know when to be cautious. (pp. 167–168)

As discussed in Chapter 1, the administrator must be able to bring about a shared vision if students are to be successful learners. In addition, a vision has to convey a vivid portrait of an outcome in enough detail so that all who read it or hear it can close their eyes and see precisely the same thing. School patrons and stakeholders must visualize all students achieving the same outcomes, and then it becomes possible for them to work toward the realization of the components of that shared vision (Sagor, 2000). At this point it is the leader's responsibility to make the distinction between a generic educational vision and an educational vision crafted specifically for the local district (Johnson, 1996).

Effective Characteristics and Behaviors That Impact Instruction and Culture

With the perception that public education was failing to meet the needs of America's students, demonstrated by failing test scores, a number of researchers went into the field of education to seek the answer to improving schools. These researchers initiated a trend that became known as *effective schools literature.* Table 2.1 summarizes their key ideas and findings.

TABLE 2.1   Research on School Culture and Improvement

Researchers	Findings
Stroll and Fink	Research on effective schools show a set of common traits between them (Stroll & Fink, 1994, p. 41)
Janzi and Leithwood	Six dimensions of leadership (Janzi & Leithwood, 1996, p. 523)
Sheppard	Principal behaviors can show positive influence on teachers (Sheppard, 1996, p. 39)
Blasé and Blasé	Principals who promote classroom instruction ■ Talk openly with teachers ■ Provide time for collaboration and professional development (Blasé & Blasé, 1999, p. 18)
Reitzug and Burrello	Leaders provide a supportive environment through ■ Giving teachers autonomy ■ Showing teachers the importance of continued growth ■ Encouraging risk taking and creativity ■ Creating teaming structures for collective responsibility (Reitzug & Burrello, 1995, pp. 48–49)
Edmonds	The effective school is ■ Orderly without being rigid ■ Quiet without being oppressing ■ Conducive to the instructional business at hand ■ One in which no child is allowed to fall behind a minimum level of achievement ■ One in which basic skills take precedence over other school activities ■ One in which the school's primary goal should be *student achievement* (Edmonds, 1979)

Bolman and Deal	Four frameworks with which leaders may function:
	■ Symbolic
	  ■ Understanding the culture of the organization
	  ■ Recognizing a shared vision
	  ■ Valuing all the norms, routines, patterns, and beliefs that exist within the organization
	■ Structural
	  ■ Assignment of tasks for workers
	  ■ A clear notion of who is in charge
	■ Political
	  ■ Leadership exists through competition and conflict
	  ■ Power exists in and among groups of special interest
	  ■ Bargaining is a tool that leadership must call on
	■ Human resource
	  ■ Recognizes individual strengths
	  ■ Identifies the needs of each individual within an organization
	  ■ Assigns people work where they can perform their best (Bolman & Deal, 1991)

TABLE 2.1   Continued

Researchers	Findings
Darling–Hammond, DuFour, and Arter	■ *Clear goals:* learners are able to see where they are headed
	■ *Self-assessment and reflection:* learners can monitor their own progress
	■ *Relevance:* new ideas and skills are directly related to the classroom
	■ *Pacing:* the learning is built on what is already known
	■ *Helpfulness:* the new learning has a quick effect on the students
	■ *Practice:* learners can safely test the new learning
	■ *Collaboration:* working with others helps the learner to deepen his/her understanding and application
	■ *Flexibility and efficiency:* the new learning fits nicely into a busy schedule
	■ *Long-term approach:* the learner is given plenty of time to practice (Arter, 2001)
Fullan	At the school level the moral imperative of the principal involves leading deep cultural change that mobilizes the passion and commitment of teachers, parents, and others to improve the learning of all students, including closing the achievement gap (Fullan, 2003, p. 41)

In summary, the effective school leader will strive to create an environment that promotes a healthy culture, and will strive to ensure the quality of the school's instructional program as well, using key strategies and behaviors. Peterson and Deal (1998) perhaps did the best job of summarizing all the literature about leadership and the school culture and instructional program with their list of the common characteristics of effective leaders. They list the following key behaviors of all effective leaders:

■ They communicate core values in what they say and do.
■ They honor and recognize those who have worked to serve students and the purpose of the school.
■ They observe rituals and traditions to support the school's heart and soul.
■ They recognize heroes and heroines and the work these exemplars accomplish.
■ They eloquently speak of the deeper mission (i.e., beyond the statement) of the school.
■ They celebrate the accomplishments of the staff, the students, and the community.
■ They preserve the focus on students by recounting stories of success and achievement. (p. 30)

Table 2.2 further summarizes the characteristics and actions of a healthy school culture, strong leadership, and a strong instructional program.

The inexorable relationship between a healthy school culture, strong leadership, and a strong instructional program is evident in everyday teaching and learning. This provides a "lens" with which to view the school or district. Reflecting on relationships between a healthy school culture, strong leadership, and a strong instructional program provides the school administrator with a powerful reflection tool.

TABLE 2.2   Summary of Characteristics

A healthy school culture actively . . .	Strong leaders actively . . .	A strong instructional program actively . . .
Promotes a climate of physical and emotional safety combined with cognitive challenges	Act through powerful policy decisions and implementations	Creates the educational direction
Emphasizes student achievement	Model the value of teaching and learning	Sets the tone for educational quality
Approaches teaching and learning with long-term goals, in that all teachers are given time to practice their skills	Purge ineffective teachers	Ensures each child reaches not only his/her academic potential, but his/her human potential
Encourages the use of collaboration as a tool for learning	Facilitate problem resolution	Encourages rigorous content within the classroom
Possesses a set of clearly defined goals, a collaborative planning process involving all staff	Provide feedback for teachers' pedagogy	Encourages curriculum development
Frames and communicates school goals to all stakeholders	Lend direct assistance to teachers	Provides alternative instructional frameworks to encourage continued teacher growth
Regularly and systematically monitors and assesses student progress	Let staff participate in shared decision making	Creates organizational structures that reduce isolation and increase teaming
Encourages a collaborative staff that regularly shares teaching skills and strategies	Provide many opportunities for reward and recognition throughout the school	Encourages the use of pacing and learning built on what is already known
Encourages teachers to talk openly about teaching and learning	Encourage people to work hard to establish and maintain good relations with parents of the students	Supports each individual teacher's pedagogy
Encourages self-assessment and reflection as a tool for growth	Model and encourage risk taking	Fosters the acceptance of group goals
Promotes the development of new, fresh ideas directly related to the classroom	Supervise and evaluate instruction	Provides individualized support for all students
Sets norms of continuous learning and improvement	Protect instructional and collaboration time for teachers	Encourages justifications of practice, giving teachers autonomy to teach in a manner that is best for them
Commits to a sense of responsibility for the learning of all students	Support professional development sessions and provide incentives for learning	Encourages active research and collaboration to increase knowledge

TABLE 2.2   Continued

A healthy school culture actively . . .	Strong leaders actively . . .	A strong instructional program actively . . .
Provides opportunities for staff reflection, collective inquiry, and sharing personal practice	Become a visible figure in classrooms for teacher professional improvement	
Includes high-quality staff development opportunities	Form a leadership team (administrators and department heads) available to discuss instruction and curricular matters	
Allows all stakeholders to develop trust and respect for one another	Identify, develop, and articulate a vision for the future	

Part 2: Key Performances, Knowledges, and Dispositions for Standard 2

Key Performances

An effective school leader will use the performances associated with Standard 2 to create a healthy school culture and a successful instructional program. This section will assist the administrator in building behaviors that demonstrate attainment of the key performances listed in Standard 2.

Performances

1. Treat all with fairness, dignity, respect
2. Recognize student and staff accomplishments
3. Use a variety of supervisory and evaluation models
4. Offer multiple opportunities to learn
5. Assess culture and climate regularly

Fairness, Dignity, and Respect

Just as in Standard 1 performances, the wise principal must model the fairness and respect of all stakeholders throughout the school community. In the performance of fairness, the effective leader treats all faculty and staff as members of a professional community. In addition, an effective leader values students and parents as essential stakeholders in the educational process. Furthermore, the effective leader is never overheard criticizing members of the school community. Discussing the actions of school–community stakeholders is different than criticizing members themselves. With regard to dignity and respect, the school leader must never exploit educational stakeholders to accomplish a selfish agenda or to seek a contrived consensus. Additionally, no matter what leaders may value as appropriate, they must invite the values, beliefs, and assumptions of school–community stakeholders to inform educational practice.

Recognize Student and Staff Accomplishments

Effective leaders know how to create a culture of appreciation. They plan surprise celebrations, acknowledge jobs well done, affirm staff and student accomplishments, and—most important—take the time personally to seek out individuals and congratulate them for a job well done. Robert Marzano (2003) suggests that effective school leaders exhibit outstanding people skills and thus produce highly successful schools. He offers a table from his national research to support his view (Table 2.3).

Notice that Marzano lists "portrays confidence in teachers" as an effective behavior or performance. Celebrating and affirming significantly conveys how much an administrator respects, admires, and appreciates the work of educators.

Use a Variety of Supervisory and Evaluation Models

Effective leaders understand that it takes time to supervise instruction effectively. Careless supervision can do a great deal of harm to an instructional program. Many teachers will attest to the ineffective principals who made an appointment to observe teaching and learning in their classrooms and then failed to come at the appointed time. Most teachers, who spent days preparing an exemplary lesson, are now left disappointed and frustrated. Additionally, cursory visits that lack meaningful time for observation accomplish little with regard to supervision.

One model for encouraging teachers to take risks with their teaching is the clinical supervision model. It is especially appropriate with new teachers or teachers seeking improvement. In this model an administrator meets informally with the teachers and asks them to discuss what they would like to improve. A mutual observation time is agreed upon and the administrator uses a "scripting" approach, meaning that the administrator only writes down what is seen and heard, without judgment. Then, immediately following the lesson, the administrator and teacher sit together and discuss how things went. The administrator establishes a tone of trust to ensure the teacher feels free to talk about what he/she would

TABLE 2.3   Effective Leader Behaviors

Behaviors Associated with an Effective Leader	Behaviors Not Associated with an Effective Leader
Makes formal observations	Has frequent staff meetings
Is accessible to discuss ideas	Uses formal rewards for good teaching
Seeks teacher input for key decisions	Reviews teachers' lesson plans
Portrays confidence in teachers	Helps solve specific instructional problems
Monitors the continuity of the curriculum	Gives feedback on specific lessons

Source: Marzano (2003).

like to improve. A mutual goal is set, and the teacher and administrator agree to work on it together. The end result is improved teaching and learning.

Other good models include coaching or external validation from the National Board for Professional Teaching Standards (NBPTS) certification. Utilizing the coaching model, "external coaches" visit the teacher's classroom and make suggestions regarding how instruction can be improved. This model is effective because the external coach has no supervisory authority over the teacher, but rather is viewed as an "expert" in a particular content area or instructional technique. Alternately, the NBPTS process is a highly effective means if taking the experienced teacher to a higher level of accomplishment. Regardless of the model used, an effective leader will always encourage the use of a multiple array of methods by offering release time, resources, grant support, and personal encouragement to the teachers willing to undertake the process of improving their teaching.

Offer Multiple Opportunities to Learn

The effective leader will provide varied and multiple forms of opportunities for staff and students to engage in learning. Too often, ineffective leaders ask faculty and staff members to take on additional responsibilities without any lessening of other responsibilities. Ineffective leadership has too often resulted in teachers hearing constant reminders of "reform," "restructure," and "renew." When none of these admonitions is offered with any real support, many teachers become overwhelmed and exhausted.

Effective leaders constantly seek external resources to support good teaching and learning. Tight school budgets often make it impossible to provide multiple opportunities to learn, but grants are a very effective way to fund such experiences. The Internet is an excellent source for grants for all kinds of school activities. The US Department of Education lists numerous grants on their website. In addition, there are more than 10,000 foundations offering funding to schools. Educators are more likely to undertake challenging new initiatives when they know that the funding is in place to support their work.

Assess Culture and Climate Regularly

As discussed earlier, Deal and Peterson (1999) have written extensively about assessing and monitoring culture. They suggest that school leaders talk with staff members who have been at the school for a long time, look over artifacts of school history, and discuss the school's past culture at staff meetings. In addition, they note that two important questions should be answered following the culture assessment steps:

1. What aspects of the culture are positive and should be reinforced?
2. What aspects of the culture are negative and harmful, and should be changed? (p. 4)

Representative Comments Demonstrating Emerging Performances for Standard 2

- "I noticed that one of your goals was to pursue a PhD and I would like to support your efforts. Let's explore how you might fulfill the residency requirement. I will help you explore a sabbatical if necessary."
- "As a master teacher, I know you self-reflect often. This is a powerful means of professional growth. How can I support your self-evaluation?"

- "I wanted to thank you for your 25 years of custodial service. A clean and well-maintained facility is essential to teaching and learning. Because of your efforts, teaching and learning are improved."
- "John, you've not offered an opinion on this topic. Given your industrial background in human relations, the committee would appreciate knowing what you are thinking."

Representative Actions Demonstrating Emerging Performances for Standard 2

- The leader considers the adequacy of resources needed to support a particular program and multiple venues, both internal and external, to ensure the program flourishes.
- The leader does not advocate a one-size-fits-all approach to professional growth, promoting multiple evaluation models.
- The leader praises both privately and publicly in ways that promote cooperation, not competition.
- The leader makes "informed" decisions by listening to and valuing multiple stakeholders, using objective criteria, and minimizing the influence of emotion.

Key Knowledges and Dispositions

Earlier in this chapter we demonstrated how an effective administrator will use the performances associated with Standard 2 to develop a healthy school culture and instructional program. In addition to performances, Standard 2 contains knowledges and dispositions. This section assists the administrator in building behaviors that demonstrate attainment of the knowledges and dispositions. The following list details those key knowledges and dispositions from Standard 2:

Knowledges
The administrator has a knowledge and understanding of

1. School cultures
2. Student growth and development
3. Applied learning theories
4. Applied motivational theories
5. Curriculum design, implementation, evaluation, and refinement
6. Principles of effective instruction
7. Measurement, evaluation, and assessment strategies
8. Diversity and its meaning for educational programs
9. Adult learning and professional development models
10. The change process for systems, organizations, and individuals
11. The role of technology in promoting student learning and professional growth

Dispositions
The administrator believes in, values, and is committed to

1. Student learning as the fundamental purpose of schooling
2. The proposition that all students can learn

3. The proposition that students learn in a variety of ways
4. Lifelong learning for self and others
5. Professional development as an integral part of school improvement
6. A safe and supportive learning environment
7. Preparing students to be contributing members of society

It is clear that the knowledges and dispositions for Standard 2 are closely aligned with the concepts presented earlier in this chapter. An effective leader understands school culture, curriculum theory, student learning, instructional strategies, and the importance of diversity. In addition, an effective leader holds clear and firm beliefs about the educability of all students, the importance of effective staff development, the recognition that not all students learn in the same way, and the need for schools to contribute to the larger community. A few examples are presented here of how building and district leaders can demonstrate their attainment of the key knowledges and dispositions established in Standard 2.

Key Knowledges

The key knowledges for Standard 2 can be summarized as the elements that combine into the general field of educational foundations, particularly in educational psychology. In other words, the knowledges needed for the attainment of Standard 2 are actually the elements related to how children and adults learn. First, children and adults cannot learn in a "toxic" culture. When the school culture is less than healthy, members of the school community do not feel valued and engaged, withdrawing from other stakeholders and withholding their creativity and work. On the other hand, when the school leader fosters a "healthy" culture in which people are valued, all the members of that community are encouraged to contribute, grow, and learn. Second, an effective school leader understands the learning theories that apply to students and adults. It is critical for the leader to understand that children learn developmentally. In addition, a wise leader knows that adults learn best when their staff development is authentic, embedded, and ongoing. Finally, an effective leader understands how to manage and provide leadership for change. As discussed in Chapter 1, change is often messy and chaotic. An effective leader will accept that change creates conflict, but will build capacities for change. These capacities will be aligned with the climate and culture of the setting, and will be sensitive to stakeholder needs.

Representative Comments Demonstrating Emerging Knowledges for Standard 2

- "I noticed that you have displayed multiple student works in the hallway. I was pleased to see that you care enough to spend all the extra time it must have taken to prepare such a fine display. I am sure your students must feel very proud to see their work presented like this."
- "I remember you mentioned to me that you're interested in the new brain research on math instruction. I'd like to encourage you to attend a workshop on this topic during the academic year and will find the resources to cover the costs. After attending, would you be willing to share your experience with the faculty?"
- "Would you like to help me with a school–community project? I believe you could provide the essential leadership necessary to make this endeavor successful. I know initiatives such as this are important to you and I would value your assistance."

- "I'm happy to approve this request to fund substitutes for the teachers in your building to attend this professional development activity; however, I would like to know how this aligns with your school improvement work."

Representative Actions Demonstrating Emerging Knowledges for Standard 2

- The leader makes special arrangements for celebrations, such as a spontaneous gathering after a support staff meeting, with refreshments and certificates marking the completion of a comprehensive project.
- The leader makes a special effort to study the school culture and determine whether it is healthy or toxic.
- The leader uses grant funds to take a team of teachers to a conference devoted to something directly related to the school improvement plan.
- The leader demonstrates a "best practice" strategy to teachers during a staff meeting.
- The leader actively promotes and encourages teachers to apply for National Board certification by advocating for necessary resources to provide release time and providing personal support.

Key Dispositions

School leaders with appropriate dispositions for Standard 2 believe that *all* children can learn. They demonstrate this belief by focusing constantly on students and their learning. There are three elements that best summarize the appropriate attitudes for Standard 2. First, great leaders are seen as always keeping the staff and parents focused on the students. They do not allow the pressures impacting schools to deviate from this student-centered focus. Second, effective leaders are seen as people who continue their professional growth. Great leaders are willing to take courses at the university, read books about improving schools, and attend staff development aimed at school effectiveness. They know that they can never learn enough. Finally, effective leaders are mentors for students and staff in the values of lifelong service to the larger community. Great leaders are known as community volunteers and activists. They are role models for students and staff in the traits of service to society.

Representative Comments Demonstrating Emerging Dispositions for Standard 2

- "We have many competing demands that must be addressed; however, at our next meeting, we must address the improvement of our instructional program. I'll arrange for the time and opportunity to deal with the other issues, but for our next meeting, I want us all to take a serious look at our instructional strategies."
- "I can see that you're really frustrated with this student's progress. Maybe we could try and build a differentiated plan for her. Let me cover your class tomorrow afternoon while you develop an individualized plan that better suits her needs. You can use my office if you want."
- "Let's meet next week and work on this new grant together. We simply must find the funds for your team to go to that national conference."
- "I'd like to see your students learning to care about their community as much as I'd like to see their test scores improve. Test scores are an important measure of success, but there are other indicators of success too."

Representative Actions Demonstrating Emerging Dispositions for Standard 2

- The leader spends extra hours during each week researching grant opportunities and making arrangements for grant submissions each year.
- The leader works with the larger community on boards or volunteer committees, listening to what the community needs and bringing this information to the school community.
- The leader works with the staff to make plans for effective staff development that is embedded, ongoing, authentic, and tied to school improvement planning.
- The leader pursues professional development by teaching courses at the university nearby; writing articles for the newspaper; and presenting at local, regional, and national conferences. These activities model lifelong learning for the school community.

The previous analysis is only a brief overview of how the standard can take on meaning in the administrator's day. The representative comments and actions are helpful when building the professional portfolio. Specific steps for building the portfolio are discussed in the next section. In addition, refer to the accompanying CD-ROM for further activities related to Standard 2.

Part 3: Portfolio Exercise for Standard 2

The following exercise will help students seeking administrative licensure to build their professional portfolios. Procedures are described here that will lead to a completed entry for a professional portfolio (Standard 2: School Culture and Instructional Program). A five-level scoring rubric to measure the level of standard attainment is contained Appendix B. The rubric provides the rater with scoring criteria to evaluate the portfolio exercise.

1. Access your file box and find the divider for Standard 2.
2. Consider the strategies of leaders who establish a healthy school culture and a successful instructional program as discussed in Chapter 2. Think about what activities a leader would use to implement these strategies. Choose one activity that you will develop in your educational setting. Examples include setting up a staff meeting to discuss a staff development proposal, compiling examples of best practices in classroom instruction and modeling them for teachers, and leading school stakeholders toward districtwide school improvement efforts. Think about the performances, knowledges, and dispositions associated with Standard 2, and discuss them in your narrative section.
3. Conduct the activity and keep a record by using a video or audio recorder.
4. Review the audio/video recording and write a reflection about what happened. The reflection should include a description of the setting (place, time, participants, etc.), what happened and why (analysis), and what you found was successful as well as what you would do differently if you had the opportunity (reflection).
5. Write about how the activity demonstrates your attainment of the standard.

6. Provide written authenticity for the activity. For example your supervisor writes a letter attesting to your performance of the activity, or a policy statement is developed or shared.

7. Place the video- or audiotape in the divider for Standard 2. Place the written samples in the folders.

8. Carefully review all items and correct any errors.

A sample cover sheet and reflection narrative follow.

BOX **2.1**

Sample Portfolio Entry

Artifact for Standard 2: School Culture and Instructional Program

Name of Artifact: Program from Reading Recognition Night

Date: May 27, 20XX

Elmwood High School

Elmwood Unified Schools

Artifact

The attached program lists the events and the names of the students being honored at a evening recognition convocation held at my high school. The purpose of this event was to celebrate the achievement of those students who excelled in advanced placement (AP) programs during the 20XX to 20XX school year and to recognize participating faculty.

Reflection Narrative

Based on the results of the statewide tests administered during the last several years, our staff identified AP programming as an academic target area to increase two- and four-year postgraduation enrollments. Only 42% of our student population scored at an acceptable level on the statewide AP tests two year ago, indicating that this is an area needing improvement. As the principal of this building, I have the responsibility of leading the staff in developing effective strategies for addressing this challenging area. I also have the responsibility of creating a climate in which success in this area is valued and celebrated.

During the first staff meeting last year, I led the staff in a discussion about strategies we could use to increase AP enrollments. One point, which was emphasized by many staff members throughout the discussion, was that "we must involve the middle school to ensure interventions are being made early on." Although the staff generally agreed that this is true, some teachers expressed that using the bell curve in AP classes discouraged students.

Following this lively discussion, I asked staff members to consider serving on a committee designed to improve AP enrollments. Concurrently, I asked AP teachers to consider the program-specific interventions needed to improve statewide scoring results. Two committees were formed and met regularly. They reported to the full staff during monthly meetings, sharing their ongoing work. Eventually a plan, which included the eighth grade teachers, was codified with support and implemented. In part, it eliminated a staunch adherence to bell curve usage, aligned AP outcomes in all content areas, and focused on recruitment in the eighth grade by offering for-credit high school classes to qualified students.

Throughout the year, staff members were encouraged to demonstrate how the changes in AP programming were making a difference, and opportunities were created to do so. The guidance department was involved to enhance recruitment and communication efforts further. A bulletin board was created in the main hallway of the school building to celebrate AP programs. At the end of the year, during the scholarship awards ceremony, AP classes were included on the agenda. Faculty members were recognized for their contributions, and students were recognized for their significant accomplishments. AP recognition met with such success, the superintendent requested AP students and staff attend the next board meeting to be recognized in a "Spotlight on Excellence" program. As a result of the school's targeted efforts, scores from last fall improved 17%, program participation has increased by 22%, and the guidance department is reporting a 19% increase in two- and four-year admissions by graduating seniors.

In analyzing the effectiveness of these efforts, I considered several factors. Our goal was to focus on AP programming as an academic target area to increase two- and four-year postgraduation enrollments. The program interventions were successful in meeting this goal, as evidenced by increased AP participation, improved statewide scores, and increased admissions in two- and four-year institutions. The staff and I agree that the interventions were successful and we will continue to evaluate programming again next year.

One of the benefits of this program has been its schoolwide implementation. The staff has worked collaboratively to ensure its success. Additionally, opportunities have been created to engage the middle school in our school improvement efforts.

Overall, I believe the interventions have improved teaching and learning. Perhaps now that we are improving AP programming, we can begin to investigate effective ways of improving other programs.

I also believe that these program interventions have positively impacted the culture of our school. Many students and their families are participating in a program once offered only to a select few. Students and parents often stop at the bulletin board to view program successes, offering praise and encouragement for participants. I plan to seek ways to extend this atmosphere of encouragement to other programs.

Scoring Analysis for the Entry

Using the portfolio exercise scoring rubric (Appendix B), this entry would score a 4. There is clear evidence of the principal's consistent efforts to improve climate and instruction in his/her school. The description is concise; it shows how program interventions were developed and linked directly to a targeted goal. The description demonstrates the impact of the program interventions on the climate of the school, although the tie to instruction efforts is less evident. The analysis shows that the principal is using multiple measurements of success of the program interventions, although data from a longer period of implementation are needed to reach meaningful conclusions. The reflection identifies a need for further program considerations and specifies the desire to broaden the successes to other programs. If the principal had shown more evidence of personal professional growth, as well as more evidence that instruction as well as climate was impacted, this entry would have scored a 5.

Suggestions for Standard 2 Sample Artifacts

- A video of the candidate conducting a staff meeting in which there is discussion of the school's climate and culture
- A video of the candidate conducting a staff meeting in which there is discussion of AP instructional programming

(continued)

BOX **2.1**   **Continued**

- Memos to the staff demonstrating a concerted effort to ensure interventions are being implemented
- A collection of varied artifacts such as bulletin board snapshots, copies of memos, newsletters, and e-mail that demonstrate the school's efforts to create a healthy climate or culture
- An audiotape of the candidate explaining to the school board how the climate/culture and instructional program for the district will be improved

---

Part 4: Case Study, Standard 2

Read the scenario that follows and answer the questions provided at the end. Sample answers to each question are provided on the enclosed CD-ROM to guide you.

Gerardo Vasquez is beginning his second year as principal of Washington High School. The chair of the social studies department has come to him with the suggestion that Washington High incorporate a service learning component into their high school program. Although Gerardo sees many potential positive outcomes from the inclusion of service learning in the curriculum, he is concerned about the reaction of staff in other departments. Also, student performance on the state's graduation exam was weak in mathematics, and the staff has been focusing its energies on raising student scores in this area. Gerardo is concerned that staff will view the implementation of a service learning component as too much effort on top of their already-overcrowded professional day. On the other hand, he was recently approached by the president of the local Chamber of Commerce, who wants to speak with him about ways to involve the business community with the school. Service learning projects may provide an avenue for such collaborations. In contemplating his portfolio entry for Standard 2, Climate and Instruction, Gerardo wonders if this would be an appropriate project for him to consider. He believes that if he can convince his full staff that the inclusion of service learning throughout the curriculum can integrate readily with the existing curriculum, can make instruction more relevant for students, and can promote higher student achievement in math, then they will strengthen the climate of the school and improve instruction. He decides to introduce the idea at a meeting of department chairs. The chair of the science department is very enthusiastic, suggesting several possible service learning projects that would integrate science, math, and language skills. The chair of the math department, however, is very resistant to the idea. She expresses the view that such a program would be "frivolous" and would "take away from the time students need doing *real* math." The chairs of the other departments seem willing to investigate the idea, although none are as enthusiastic as the science chair. Following this meeting, Gerardo meets with the chairs of the science and social studies departments. They agree to work together to develop a proposal for a pilot project that integrates service learning with the standards in science, math, and social studies (specifically, civics and government).

Question 1: As Gerardo guides his staff through an exploration of developing a service learning component for the high school curriculum, what artifacts might he consider collecting for his portfolio? How could he best document this process so a portfolio reviewer will understand both the process and his role in the process?

Question 2: Put yourself in Gerardo's place. Write a brief description of the reaction of the other chairs to the proposal. Identify and analyze any resistance you might encounter and the reasons for this resistance. Finally, write a reflection about your role in this process. What have you done, and what can you do in the future, to impact climate and instruction in your building through this service learning proposal?

Question 3: What performances, knowledges, and dispositions related to Standard 2 could Gerardo document using this project? Is this a good choice for Standard 2? Why or why not?

3 Standard 3: Management

Management controls, arranges, does things right; leadership unleashes energy, sets the vision so we do the right thing.

—Bennis & Nanus, 1985

A school administrator is an educational leader who promotes the success of all students and staff by ensuring management of the organization, operations, and resources for a safe, efficient, and effective learning environment.

OBJECTIVES

The learner will

- Understand the historical context of management theory
- Understand the key performances, knowledges, and dispositions for Standard 3
- Practice completing a portfolio entry for Standard 3
- Interact with a case study to reflect on putting Standard 3 into action

Part 1: Examining Standard 3

Management Theory Then and Now

A review of the early and contemporary theories of organizational management theory is a prerequisite to developing a portfolio entry based on the management standard. To meet the requirements of Standard 3, a school administrator must know how to "promote the success of all students and staff by ensuring management of the organization, operations, and resources for a safe, efficient, and effective learning environment" (Appendix A, Standard 3). The ability to manage the complex organization of a school or district is multifaceted and requires knowledge of management theory and practical management skills.

Management in school leadership is often viewed unenthusiastically by many individuals because it brings to mind issues such as the management details associated with budgeting, transportation, collective bargaining/negotiations, school construction, and facilities—topics often considered not very exciting when compared with instructional leadership, school–community relations, or building vision. Although *creativity* and *vision* are not terms traditionally associated with management theory, their recognition and use by school leaders in making management decisions enhances all the other leadership characteristics and standards presented in this text. Without effective and efficient management of the educational organization, its operations, and its resources, school leaders will find it difficult if not impossible to transform and lead their schools or school districts. As Ménendez–Morse (1992) points out, the central theme of the research on leaders versus managers is that "those who find themselves supervising people in an organization should be both good managers and good leaders" (p. 3).

To develop a complete understanding and appreciation for management concepts, this part of the chapter provides a historical context and updates the reader on current practices. Owens (1987) delineates four phases in the development of administrative theory: classical organizational theory (1910–1935), human relations (1935–1950), organizational behavior (1950–1975), and human resources management (1975–present). Other theorists (e.g., Hoy & Miskel, 1987; Marion, 2002) depict the eras with similar terminology and slightly different dates, but in general these four phases in the development of management theory are widely recognized by scholars and practitioners. Viewing these eras in the development of management theory as being closed or open is another categorization that is important and is emphasized in this summary. Because introductory educational administration texts provide a detailed account of management theory, highlights of the theories are outlined in Table 3.1 and are briefly discussed in the sections that follow. The reader is en-

TABLE 3.1   Summary of Management Theories

Theory	Contentions
Classical management theory (1910–1935)	Includes scientific management, administration management, and bureaucracy theory within the closed system structure. Theories maintain that organizations are self-contained entities largely untainted by external forces or issues, and that efficiency is served by controlling internal activities.
Human relations movement (1935–1950)	Relates organizational performance to personal and social needs and behaviors. Emphasizes human and interpersonal factors in managing an organization: It is a closed system structure due to its assumption of efficiency and effectiveness.
Organizational behavior movement (1950–1975)	Seeks to describe, understand, and predict human behavior in formal organizations. It reflects open systems theory.
Human resources management (1975–present)	Views organizations as energizing, productive, and rewarding for their participants. It reflects open systems theory.

couraged to investigate the original works to explore the additional factors not presented in the management theory summaries.

Classical Management Theory (1910–1935)

The era of classical management theory is also referred to as part of the *closed systems organizational theory*. According to Marion (2002), "closed systems" theory "gets its name from the underlying presumption that organizations are self-contained entities largely untainted by external forces or issues, and that efficiency is served by controlling internal activities" (p. 2). He reminds us that the closed systems perspective was in place during the development of modern school culture, with its influence on schools still in evidence today. Marion (2002) includes the fields of scientific management, administration management, and bureaucracy theory within the closed systems structure.

Much of what leaders do is strongly rooted in the assumptions, values, and practices of scientific management. This makes it extremely difficult for schools, and indeed most organizations today, to break free from the inherent view of reality suggested by this management theory.

Human Relations Movement (1935–1950)

Human relations theory relates organizational performance to personal and social needs and behaviors. It seeks to understand those behaviors and to increase organizational productivity with effective human relations intervention (Marion, 2002). Marion (2002) makes it clear, however, that although human relations theory is more sensitive to environmental influences, it is still classified as a closed system because of its assumption of efficiency and effectiveness.

The human relations movement emphasized human and interpersonal factors in managing an organization. However, one of the criticisms of this theory is the potential perception of manipulation by management. Owens (1987) concludes that the human relations movement had minimal impact on superintendents, but that it did have substantial impact on supervisory personnel (district-level supervisors and school principals). He shares that, in general, superintendents continued to focus on hierarchical control, authority, and formal organization, whereas supervisory personnel embraced human relations concepts such as morale building, group cohesiveness, collaboration, and the dynamics of informal organization.

Organizational Behavior Movement (1950–1975)

Several researchers and their books built the framework for the organizational behavior movement. Chester Barnard's *The Functions of the Executive* (published in 1938), Felix Roethlisberger and William Dickson's *Management and the Worker* (1939), and Herbert Simon's *Administrative Behavior* (1947) set the theoretical foundation for the study of organizational behavior as a discipline to describe, understand, and predict human behavior in formal organizations (Owens, 1987).

It was at this point in history that Owens (1987) indicates that a change in the field of educational administration was brewing. He observes that prior to the mid 1950s, courses in educational administration focused on teaching future administrators how to solve practical problems, and rarely used theory to explain practice. Furthermore, prior to the mid 1950s, research in the field consisted primarily of conducting status studies of current programs or soliciting opinions. There was little, if any, research that tested theory, and none of it involved using behavioral science research methods. By the mid 1950s, however, Owens (1987) states:

> A new concept of organization was gaining wide acceptance among students of educational administration. This new concept recognized the dynamic interrelationships between (1) the structural characteristics of the organization and (2) the personal characteristics of the individual. It sought to understand the behavior of people at work in terms of the dynamic interrelationships between the organizational structure and the people who populated it. (p. 20)

Instead of being viewed as being unaffected by external forces, organizations such as school districts and schools were now being conceptualized as social systems. Marion (2002) considers this new conceptualization as the next logical step in the evolution of organization theory—*open systems theory*. Open systems theory became popular during the 1960s, and Marion (2002) states that it "made the then revolutionary claim that organizational structure and behavior are significantly influenced by their environments" (p. 86). Hence, organizational theory reached the stage at which educational leaders were able to identify with the theories and draw insights that applied to their everyday activities. Both the organizational behavior era and human resources management era are viewed within the open systems perspective.

Human Resources Management (1975–present)

According to Owens (1987), a fourth approach to organizational management evolved in the mid 1980s—human resources management. The human resources perspective views organizations as energizing, productive, and rewarding for their participants (Bolman & Deal, 1997, as cited in Razik & Swanson, 2001). They list the basic assumptions of the model as follows:

- Organizations exist to serve human needs rather than the reverse.
- People and organizations need each other.
- When the fit between the individual and the system is poor, both suffer.
- A good fit profits both the individual and the organization.

These practices include

- Hiring right and rewarding well
- Providing security for employees
- Promoting from within
- Providing training and education for employees
- Sharing the wealth with the workers (p. 90)

Sergiovanni and colleagues (1992) conclude that human resources theories reflect not only an interest in people at work, but also a new regard for their potential. Examples they give include viewing teachers as professionals able to respond to progressive, optimizing ideas, such as shared decision making, joint planning, common goals, increased responsibility, and job enrichment. They see the educational manifestation of these human resources concepts in team teaching, family grouping, open space, school within a school, open corridor, integrated day, and multiunit. In their opinion, the human resources view of administration places a great deal of emphasis on autonomy, inner direction, and the desire for maximum self-development at work. This view of organizations should familiarize the reader with the current stream of thought concerning organizations, people that work in them, and their leaders.

Implications

Chapter 1 of this book discussed the emergence of new theories of educational leadership in the 1990s and depicted them as values-laden professional relationships. These theories and ideas concerning leadership all evolved from earlier theories of organizations and management, with the greatest emphasis on the human relations and human resources aspects covered in the previous sections. However, an educational leader must have a wide view of leadership theory and must be able to reflect on how the theories relate and interact with each other, then determine how to put all the pieces together to develop a personal leadership perspective. One thing all the new theories of leadership have in common is an emphasis on the human, emotional side of leadership. Indeed, having people skills is an essential ingredient for success and one that every leader should possess; however, the task or management side of the equation cannot be neglected. People skills alone will not get an administrator out of trouble with the superintendent or school board if there is a budget shortfall, or if the school plant and operations are not managed effectively and efficiently, and in a way that maximizes student learning. With this in mind, Part 2 of this chapter turns to a discussion of the key performances, knowledges, and dispositions associated with Standard 3.

Part 2: Key Performances, Knowledges, and Dispositions for Standard 3

Key Performances

Although Part 1 of this chapter provided a historical context for understanding management and organizational theory, Part 2 will present these theories, showing their relationship to practice in managing the organization, its operations, and its resources. The key elements of this standard are *management of the organization and operations* and *providing resources for a safe, effective learning environment*. Each of these elements is discussed in this section along with evidence supporting their importance in the overall vision and leadership of the school and/or district.

The 22 performance standards listed here are of primary concern because they are the most obvious manifestation of the management standard in action. An administrator's success or failure to manage the school organization is measured primarily by others (e.g., teachers, students, parents, superintendent, school board, the community). The management performance standards are comprehensive in scope, ranging from the knowledge of learning, teaching, and student development, to managing fiscal resources effectively, as well as being an effective time manager, problem solver, communicator, negotiator, and entrepreneur. Hence, successful demonstration of the performances not only for the management standard, but also for the others, provides outward evidence of an administrator's ability to lead or not lead the school organization effectively and efficiently while developing and promoting its vision. The five distinct phases of standards attainment (introductory, developmental, proficiency, maintenance and renewal, and assessment) outlined in the introduction of the book are important considerations when assessing an administrator's attainment of the performance standards in this section. It will likely take a minimum of five years for an individual to become proficient in all the performances associated with the management standard.

Performances

1. Knowledge of learning, teaching, and student development is used in reaching management decisions
2. Operational procedures are designed and managed to maximize opportunities for successful learning
3. Emerging trends are recognized, studied, and applied as appropriate
4. Operational plans and procedures to achieve the vision and goals of the school are in place
5. Collective bargaining and other contractual agreements related to the school are effectively managed
6. The school plant, equipment, and support systems operate safely, efficiently, and effectively
7. Time is managed to maximize attainment of organizational goals
8. Potential problems and opportunities are identified
9. Problems are confronted and resolved in a timely manner
10. Financial, human, and material resources are aligned to the goals of the school
11. The school acts entrepreneurially to support continuous improvement
12. Organizational systems are regularly monitored and modified as needed
13. Stakeholders are involved in decisions affecting schools
14. Responsibility is shared to maximize ownership and accountability
15. Effective problem-framing and problem-solving skills are used
16. Conflict is effectively managed
17. Effective group process and consensus-building skills are used
18. Effective communication skills are used
19. There is effective use of technology to manage school operations
20. Fiscal resources of the school are managed responsibly, efficiently, and effectively
21. A safe, clean, and aesthetically pleasing school environment is created and maintained
22. Confidentiality and privacy of school records are maintained

It is interesting to note how often the terms *managed* and *effective* are used in the listing of these key performances. The lasting impact of classical management theory (or the closed systems theory) is still very evident in the current educational arena. Marion (2002) stresses the fact that "no matter how 'modern' and sophisticated our theories have become, we cannot escape the necessity for efficient and effective production, whether that production is cars or education" (p. 22). In the current climate of increased accountability, accomplished leaders understand and practice efficient and effective management of the educational organization, in concert with providing leadership that develops and implements a vision of teaching and learning that is shared by all.

According to Sergiovanni, Burlingame, Coombs, and Thurston (1992), in education, modern scientific management offers efficiency ideas such as "performance contracting, behavioral objectives, state and national assessment, **cost–benefit analysis**, management by objective, planning programming budgeting system, and management information systems each prescribed to maximize education reliability and productivity at deceased cost" (p. 133). Many of these management techniques are computerized. Learning how to utilize them entails both learning how to use the software and learning how to interpret the results. Hence, it appears that the use of modern scientific management (with its focus on efficiency) in combination with the human resources management theory (with its focus on the individual), allows the educational organization to thrive because the needs of the organization and the individual are met simultaneously. Thus, the key is developing leaders who are capable of not only tackling the management and human issues, but also addressing them with finesse and fortitude so that difficult decisions are made for the good of the organization. For example, dismissal of an insubordinate teacher is a difficult task, but one that is necessary if the vision and success of the school is paramount. Indeed, employment issues impact the efficiency and effectiveness of the school and must be given attention when they impact student learning. However, it must be done in a manner in which the individuals involved are treated professionally, with concern and compassion. Hence, the new theories of leadership presented in Chapter 1 that emphasize relationships and a values orientation are important to keep in mind, because they should be at the heart of how school leaders think and act in the twenty-first century.

Managing the organization, its operations, and resources while simultaneously providing leadership that emphasizes the human side of change and the importance of emotional intelligence and values-laden professional relationships as presented in Chapter 1 is not an easy undertaking. Although management and leadership are often viewed as two distinct characteristics, it is possible to be an effective manager and outstanding leader as long as one is:

- Aware of the components necessary to perform both roles
- Able to demonstrate these performances consistently in practice
- Able to listen to others
- Willing to fail and try again

It is important to realize that the competencies associated with the standards are not learned and demonstrated overnight. It takes several years to develop proficiency and then to maintain these competencies throughout one's career. Ongoing professional development, even for seasoned administrators, is a prerequisite for continued success on the job. New theories are developed, reform initiatives are altered, and today's technology and software are quickly outdated. Therefore, maintaining the status quo is not sufficient for leading and managing today's schools. Administrators must be constantly updating their skills and knowledge of leadership and management to remain current.

Representative Comments Demonstrating Emerging Performances for Standard 3

- "What can we do to make better use of technology to manage utility costs, maintenance operations, and custodial services at our school?"
- "Does block scheduling help maximize opportunities for successful learning? Let's investigate the research literature before we consider this option."
- "Although turning off the air conditioning at 1:00 PM might save some money, the comfort of the students to maximize their learning is more important."
- "How can we generate extra funds to support the academic program?"
- "I will make sure the problem with the leak in your ceiling is reported immediately."
- "The collective bargaining agreement permits teachers to sponsor extracurricular activities. Who is willing to sponsor a club?"
- "What is the maximum use of my time right now?"

Representative Actions Demonstrating Emerging Performances for Standard 3

- The principal communicates with the local business community to garner support for school activities that the general fund budget is unable to support.
- As appropriate, the principal compliments the custodians and district maintenance workers after they have completed a project or finished their assigned work.
- The principal ensures that all school records are safely stored and that access is restricted to appropriate personnel. An access sheet is maintained for each student record.
- The principal effectively manages the school resources and maximizes the efficiency of each dollar spent.
- The principal subscribes to several education journals to keep abreast of current research on student learning, teaching, and student development.

Key Knowledges and Dispositions

Previously this chapter demonstrated how an effective administrator will use the performances associated with Standard 3 to develop a management pedagogy. In addition to performances, Standard 3 contains knowledges and dispositions. This section will assist the administrator in building behaviors that demonstrate attainment of the knowledges and dispositions. The following lists detail the key knowledges and dispositions from Standard 3:

Knowledges
The administrator has a knowledge and understanding of

1. Theories and models of organizations, and the principles of organizational development
2. Human resources management and development
3. Operational policies and procedures at the school and district levels

4. Principles and issues relating to school safety and security
5. Principles and issues relating to fiscal operations of school management
6. Principles and issues relating to school facilities and use of space
7. Legal issues impacting school operations
8. Current technologies that support management functions

Dispositions
The administrator believes in, values, and is committed to

1. Making management decisions to enhance learning and teaching
2. Accepting responsibility
3. High-quality standards, expectations, and performances
4. Involving stakeholders in management processes
5. Cultivating a safe and trusting environment

Key Knowledges

The old saying "knowledge is power" is why the knowledge items associated with each standard are essential in the development of school leaders. Without background knowledge of the job functions (i.e., essential knowledge components), leaders are unable to operate at full capacity. Even if someone else is assigned responsibility for the job function, the ultimate responsibility for its successful accomplishment lies with the leader. To know whether something in the school facility is operating properly, or whether policies related to school safety and security are being implemented as intended, the school administrator must have knowledge and understanding of the principles and issues related to these areas. Likewise, if the school administrator is not aware of the legal issues that impact school operations, the possibility of making costly mistakes is likely. In dealing with everyday legal issues that impact school operations, a working knowledge of education law—which includes knowledge of tort liability, special education legal matters, and labor and employment laws—should be sufficient to determine when help is needed. The best advice offered by Weeks (2001) is to not play lawyer. He contends that effective school management necessitates the retention of good, experienced legal counsel. Most school districts retain a school attorney, so if there are any questions or problems either at the school or district levels, contacting the school attorney is advised.

Fiscal operations of school management are clear-cut, but are often the source of controversy. A trusted and competent bookkeeper at the school level and an experienced school business manager or treasurer at the district level is a leadership imperative. Yet, in small schools or districts, fiscal responsibility often falls on the principal or superintendent. Therefore, building- and district-level administrators should have knowledge and understanding of topics such as strategic planning and budgeting, accounting, auditing, and reporting. District administrators would add the areas of personnel and payroll administration, purchasing and distribution, maintenance and operation, capital asset planning and management, cash management, risk management, and insurance to the list of topics in which they should demonstrate proficiency. Again, although someone else may assume the job function, the school leader assumes ultimate responsibility for success or failure. Success is rarely celebrated in fiscal management; however, failures are almost always publicized and jobs are often lost when an administrator is negligent in paying attention to the fiscal problems of the organization. Hence, knowledge and understanding of the management standard is essential for initial and continued school leader success. It is highly recommended that aspiring administrators take a course in school business management that provides both building- and district-level perspectives on the myriad of fiscal management, because there are complex issues associated with each topic that can only be dealt with in a course specifically designed for that purpose.

Although a specific course in school business management is highly recommended, it is useful to cover some fundamental school finance and budgeting essentials here. Because emerging administrators have little fiscal experience, the primary focus will be to inform a building-level administrator.

School Finance Fundamentals.   How are schools funded? Most citizens are aware that local property taxes are a source of funding for education in most states, but many do not know that there is a complex array of state-level funding formulas as well as federal sources of revenue that schools receive. Some school finance basics that school leaders should have in their repertoire include an understanding of school finance litigation, frameworks for assessing the **equity** and adequacy of school finance systems, the sources of revenue for schools and the system of taxation to support schools, funding formula options and needs adjustments, and how to use education dollars more wisely to improve results. Although these areas are not specifically mentioned in the standards, they are important concepts of which school leaders need to have a clear and comprehensive understanding to be a well-informed school leader who is proactive in ensuring the best possible education for students. As spokesperson for the school, the principal is expected to be an expert and to provide school stakeholders with timely and accurate information. For example, when the school district proposes building a new facility and the citizens in the community object to having their taxes raised to pay for its construction, the principal should be able to provide school patrons with a clear and concise outline of how their tax dollars will benefit students. This type of presentation requires knowledge in the areas of school finance basics mentioned earlier in this section.

The Education Finance Statistics Center (2004) website, which is part of the National Center for Education Statistics, is an excellent source of information concerning school funding. It has a wealth of publications and graphics, and has a peer search feature that allows a comparison of school districts with similar characteristics. A school leader is well advised to consult this website to gain additional information on school finance and other related topics.

Budgeting Basics.   How do school districts and schools budget the money they are allocated? Again, individual states differ in what they require for budgeting documents, but the essentials of good budgeting are universal. As defined by Brimley and Garfield (2002), a budget is a financial plan that contains at least four elements: planning, receiving funds, spending funds, and evaluating results. More than four decades ago, Roe (1961) defined the educational budget "as the translation of educational needs into a financial plan which is interpreted to the public in such a way that when formally adopted it expresses the kind of educational program the community is willing to support, financially and morally, for a one-year period" (p. 81). Brimley and Garfield (2002) propose the following steps for developing a financial plan: (1) identifying needs, (2) establishing goals, (3) organizing objectives, (4) building a program to meet those objectives, and (5) providing a budget to fund those programs. A district administrator is responsible for the overall budget for the school district; however, building-level administrators play a key role in contributing their piece of the budget to the district's financial plan. The same steps for developing a financial plan at the district level apply to developing a school-level budget. Unless school-based budgeting is practiced, building-level administrators often have little control over the school budget; however, they should exercise the same sound principles of planning for use of those minimal funds as they would for a larger sum. In addition, development of the financial plan should be participative and should involve school stakeholders in the process. Hence, teachers, students, parents, and community organizations should be included on a district- and school-level budget committee.

An excellent presentation of the basics of school budgeting is found in the Charlotte Advocates for Education (2004) *Community Guide to Understanding the School Budget.* This document presents the essential budget information in a format that is geared to the community. After providing an overview of the school community, it explains where the money comes from, where it goes, what the budget buys, and then offers ways community members can take action, and resources they can consult for more information. This guide could be adapted to other schools and districts, and could be used to provide school stakeholders with similar information tailored to their individual circumstances.

Representative Comments Demonstrating Emerging Knowledges for Standard 3

- "The transportation policy does not allow us to pick up your child at a location other than the school zone where you live."
- "We cannot use the school activity fund for the Spanish Club to pay for your professional development activity."
- "The playground equipment must meet the guidelines for safety outlined in the policy manual."

Representative Actions Demonstrating Emerging Knowledges for Standard 3

- The principal consults with the superintendent and school board attorney to determine whether the school can rent the basketball court to a Satanic cult for an evening each month.
- The principal attends a workshop offered by the state Association of School Business Officials on school safety and legal issues.
- The principal reviews the teacher dismissal policy to determine the process required to dismiss a teacher who is not performing his job to the required standard.

Key Dispositions

How can school leaders learn a management disposition? The first step, of course, is to be aware of the dispositions and then work toward exhibiting them in practice. It is difficult to assess management dispositions, because one can profess that one believes in, values, and is committed to the five dispositions for Standard 3, but how does an outsider know whether an individual does or does not have these dispositions? The old adage that "actions speak louder than words" hits the nail on the head. It is not what one says, but how one acts and conducts business on a daily basis that reflects one's values. What school leaders do and say should reflect the same values. For example, an administrator can profess to value involving stakeholders in the management process, but independently and without input from students, teachers, and/or parents, may decide to close the indoor pool to students and the community after school hours to avoid safety and security problems. This administrator, in this case, is not involving stakeholders in the management process. If the school bookkeeper leaves town suddenly and funds from the school accounts are mysteriously low, and a police investigation reveals that the bookkeeper has been stealing money from the accounts for more than a year, who is ultimately responsible? The building or district administrator is the overseer of the fiscal operations of the school and supervision of the staff (in this case the bookkeeper). If something goes wrong, the school leader is the one who did not keep a close enough eye on the accounts to detect the problem when it first occurred. A more positive example of cultivating a safe and trusting environment and involving stakeholders would be evident in working on a new student discipline policy with a committee of students, teachers, and parents, for which their input is considered and consensus is reached in drafting the document. Again, the emphasis should always be on making sure the school leader's words and actions are in concert with each other.

How do management dispositions in practice relate to theory? In many ways, current theories of transactional leadership theory resemble some of the components of scientific management. For example, Bennis and Nanus (1985) and Zaleznik (1989) referred to persons exhibiting the characteristics of transactional leadership as *managers*. Bass (1985) defined transactional leaders as those who saw what their followers wanted and tried to get it for them if their performance merited it, exchanged promises of rewards for certain levels of effort, and responded to the wants and needs of their subordinates so long as their efforts merited that attention. Downton (1973) applied the term *transactional* to leadership to describe an interaction wherein both leader and follower were viewed as bargaining agents trying to maximize their rewards.

Although the transactional approach to leadership appears to be a "good fit" for the management standard, in today's educational reform era, transformational leadership is highly valued and practiced. Burns (1978) proposed that transformational leadership was an extension of ordinary transactional leadership. He noted that world-class leaders obtained more from their followers than could ever be explained by a cost–benefit analysis. Therefore, a school administrator who believes in, values, and is committed to the dispositions associated with the management standard listed earlier is characterized as not only a good manager, but a visionary leader who has the best interest of students, teachers, and the community in mind when making management decisions. As emphasized earlier, personal reflection of the relationship and values-laden theories presented in Chapter 1, along with the organizational management theories provided in this chapter, should lead to the development of one's own individual views of management and leadership. Developing these perspectives of management and leadership are key ingredients for developing and maintaining a successful career as a school administrator.

Representative Comments Demonstrating Emerging Dispositions for Standard 3

- "We are going to buy the computers and software you have requested for remediation. Research and the experience of other principals using the program show it has the potential to increase reading and math scores by 30%."
- "It is my fault that your request for the field trip was delayed. The uncertainty of the availability of parents to help with the outing made me hesitant to grant permission. Now that you have six parents who have agreed to help, I will sign off on the request."
- "Our budget reflects many changes, including reallocation based on the 'adequacy' of resources for student needs."

Representative Actions Demonstrating Emerging Dispositions for Standard 3

- With the involvement of key stakeholders, the principal develops a school crisis plan and seeks approval of the faculty and staff before presenting it to the superintendent and school board for approval.
- The school's mission and vision statements are displayed at the school entrance, and in the auditorium, gymnasium, and school office. Teachers and students are reminded during the daily announcements of the standards, expectations, and performances required to make the mission and vision a reality.
- The district leader ensures expenditures from the budget reflect the district's vision and mission.

Specific steps for building the portfolio are discussed in the next section. In addition, refer to the accompanying CD-ROM for further activities related to Standard 3.

Part 3: Portfolio Exercise for Standard 3

The following exercise will help students seeking administrative licensure to build their professional portfolio. Procedures are described here that will lead to a completed entry for a professional portfolio (Standard 3). A five-level scoring rubric to measure the level of the standard attainment is contained in Appendix B. The rubric provides the rater with scoring criteria to evaluate the portfolio exercise.

1. Access your file box and find the divider for Standard 3.
2. Think about some ways that you could manage the organization, its operations, and school or school district resources to promote the success of all students in an efficient and effective learning environment. Choose an activity that would demonstrate your competence in this area. Some examples might include working with teachers and other stakeholders on determining how to spend the school budget allocation, developing a school safety/disaster plan that is in concert with the school vision and goals, or instituting a capital campaign to fund additions to the school facility. Think about the knowledges, performances, and dispositions associated with Standard 3 and discuss them in your narrative section.
3. Conduct the activity you select and document how it was enacted (digital recording, journal entries, etc.).

4. Once the activity is complete, review your documentation and reflect on what happened and how it relates to Standard 3. The reflection should include a narrative description of what you did, who was involved, when it occurred, and the outcome. On reflection, what would you do differently if you had the opportunity to perform the activity again?
5. Write about how the activity shows partial attainment of Standard 3.
6. Place the documentation with your record of the activity in one folder. Place the reflections and authenticity evidence (e.g., your supervisor writes a letter attesting to your performance of the activity, or a policy statement is developed or shared) in the two remaining folders.
7. Carefully review all the items and correct any errors.

A sample cover sheet and reflection narrative follow.

BOX **3.1**

Sample Portfolio Entry

Artifact for Standard 3: Management

Names of Artifacts: Lakeview School Crisis Plan, letter from director of Adams County Emergency Management Team, letter to Adams County Sheriff, article from *Adams County Courier* (March 17, 20XX)

Date: April 2, 20XX

Lakeview Middle School

Adams County Schools

Artifacts
These artifacts illustrate my role in coordinating the development of our schoolwide crisis management plan. The letter from the sheriff highlights his role in this collaborative process. The letter from the director of the Adams County Emergency Management Team documents the planning of a drill to test the efficacy of the plan. The newspaper article reports on the drill. The final document, the Lakeview School Crisis Plan, reflects the revisions made to our plan following the drill.

Reflection Narrative
Following the events of September 11, 2001, all principals in the Adams County School District were directed by the superintendent to oversee the development of a crisis management plan for their buildings. I led the team that developed such a plan for Lakeview Middle School, a facility that serves 240 students in grades 6 to 8. Lakeview Middle School is located on a campus that includes a high school, an elementary school, an administrative center, and a warehouse/transportation facility. (Our school district serves a rural population spread over a large but sparsely populated area.)

To initiate the development of a crisis management plan, I assembled a team of school personnel to assist with the process. This team included the nurse, the secretary, the building mainte-

(continued)

BOX **3.1**   **Continued**

nance supervisor, the head of the guidance department, a staff member from each department, and the cafeteria supervisor. The team addressed many issues. As a group, we developed "chains of command and communication" for various emergency scenarios, along with descriptions of the responsibilities of every staff member in the various crisis situations. We planned for various situations, including maintaining students in a secure environment within the building, early dismissal from the building under emergency conditions, and evacuation of the entire building to off-site locations (e.g., to the high school in the event of an in-building emergency or to the YMCA facility located two miles from campus in the event of an emergency requiring the evacuation of the entire campus).

Once this team had developed a skeletal plan, I consulted with various district and community resources to complete the process. This necessitated meetings with the director of busing to develop a plan for evacuating students, the district food service coordinator, to create a plan for feeding students and staff, if necessary; the director of the YMCA, to plan for an alternate evacuation site; and the sheriff, to develop an appropriate communication plan in the event of an emergency.

After the plan was established and approved by the superintendent, the sheriff, and the director of the county emergency management team, it was presented to the full staff, including all food service, maintenance, and transportation personnel. At this staff meeting, the sheriff's department provided additional staff training in emergency management.

To test the efficacy of the plan, I worked with the director of the county emergency management team to plan a drill. The scenario for the simulation was an explosion in the basement of the school building. I coordinated with the sheriff's department, who oversaw closing routes of traffic to the building and providing security for the site; the county emergency management team, which worked with the gas company, fire department, hospitals, and other emergency personnel; and the transportation department, which provided buses to relocate students to the high school on the far side of the campus. The drill was successful because it highlighted the parts of the plan that worked well, along with a few areas that needed revision.

The process of developing this plan, and the resultant document, are evidence of my continuing professional development in the areas addressed by Standard 3, Management. I worked successfully with building and district personnel at all levels, as well as with resource people from various community agencies, to create this plan.

Following the simulation/drill, I conducted two debriefing meetings. The first meeting was with school personnel. A few staff members indicated confusion about their roles in a crisis situation. Based on their feedback, I revised the crisis plan to include more detailed lists of the specific responsibilities of each staff member. Another area of concern was the plan for dismissing students under an emergency scenario. The building crisis management team will meet in the near future to rework these procedures to make them more efficient. The second debriefing meeting included our superintendent, the sheriff, the director of transportation for Adams County schools, and the director of the county emergency management team. Although all agencies were pleased with the drill and felt the crisis plan worked successfully, I expressed my concern about media relations. I feel we need to designate one person as a contact for all media queries so that consistent information is being provided to all parties. This is another area that will be addressed by our building team at our next meeting.

I think one of the strengths of this plan is the development of clear and specific chains of command and communication. A well-defined role is spelled out for every staff member. I was pleased with the reactions of the staff during the simulation; nearly everyone fulfilled their assigned responsibilities in an appropriate and timely fashion. Another strength is the involvement of the various emergency and resource agencies within the community. By making them part of the planning process, we all came to a better understanding of the unique needs and problems faced by the others. This allowed us to address these problems before we encountered them in an actual emergency situation. I believe this will enable the school to work more effectively with these agencies in the event of a real crisis.

I see one particular weakness in the plan now that we have tested it using the simulation. We have not planned adequately for the needs of students and staff who may need medical attention during an emergency. I intend to offer training to all staff members in first aid and CPR, and will encourage every staff member to take advantage of this training. I will participate in the first session myself. Overall, I think the development of this plan will result in greater safety for students and staff.

Scoring Analysis for the Entry
Using the portfolio exercise scoring rubric (Appendix B), this entry would score a 5. There is clear evidence of the principal's consistent efforts to manage the organization and operations of the building effectively, as well as the resources of the district and community, to ensure a safe environment for students and staff. The description is clear and detailed; it shows how the plan was developed and specifies how the principal involved all the stakeholders in the development and implementation of the plan. The analysis and reflection address both the strengths and weaknesses of the plan, and show that the principal continues to seek ways to improve the plan. The reflection identifies a need for further staff training and specifies a plan for addressing this need. A specific course of action is identified for the next steps in the process.

Suggestions for Standard 3 Sample Artifacts
- A copy of a plan of action created by the staff to deal with safety issues such as fire drills, terrorist attacks, and other catastrophic events
- A video showing the candidate leading the staff in a plan for data-driven school improvement
- Copies of various school communications showing the expertise of the candidate in managing the everyday activities of the school
- A report to the school board outlining a strategic plan to improve pupil achievement in the district
- A report to the superintendent outlining a plan for school safety

---

Part 4: Case Study, Standard 3

Read the scenario that follows and answer the questions at the end. Sample answers to each question are provided on the enclosed CD-ROM to guide you.

Marcus Jackson has just become the principal of a large, urban middle school. During his first month on the job, several parents and community members, as well as the local police chief, expressed concerns about an upsurge in vandalism within the community. Marc has noticed widespread evidence of vandalism of school property, including graffiti painted on both interior and exterior walls of the building, broken windows, damage to furniture in the school cafeteria, and destruction of landscaping on the grounds. The maintenance supervisor has complained about the amount of time he and his staff spend cleaning up after vandals and has threatened to transfer to another building if "something isn't done about this." Marc believes that a team that includes all involved parties, including students, faculty, maintenance staff, parents, and community members, should develop the solution to the problem. However, his attempt to assemble such a team met with resistance. None of the faculty responded to his request for volunteers to serve on this committee. The parents he contacted all declined his invitation to join, stating that they did not have time. The one local businessman who responded took the position that the only acceptable solution was increased security, followed by jail time for any apprehended offenders. His attitude alienated the students, who walked out of the meeting. Marc has decided to draft a plan himself for dealing with the vandalism, then ask for feedback from the school community. He intends to unveil his plan at an evening forum to which students, parents, staff, and community members will be invited. After he shares his plan, he intends to request input from the audience.

> *Question 1:* Is this problem/activity/event a good choice for Marc to make for his portfolio entry for Standard 3, Management? Why or why not? What performances, knowledges, and dispositions related to Standard 3 could Marc document using this project? Be specific.
>
> *Question 2:* What could Marc have done differently to achieve his desired outcome of having all involved parties take ownership in the problem and in finding a solution to the problem? Assuming he followed your suggestions, what artifacts would you recommend Marc collect to document his attainment of Standard 3?
>
> *Question 3:* Create a chart or list of statements Marc could use in writing about this event for his portfolio. Include statements for all three types of writing: description (What happened?), analysis (Why does it matter?), and reflection (What is the implication for the future? Where do I go from here?).

Standard 4: Collaboration with Families and the Community

4

Educators would make schools better places for more children if they thought of what they did in schools as "entering relationships" rather than as "assuming roles."

—Noddings, as cited in Larson & Ovando, 2001, p. 190

A school administrator is an educational leader who promotes the success of all students by collaborating with families and community members, responding to diverse community interests and needs, and mobilizing community resources.

OBJECTIVES

The learner will

- Understand the importance of collaboration and relationship building
- Understand the importance of effective communication
- Learn how to put Standard 4 into practice
- Reflect on the knowledges, performances, and dispositions associated with Standard 4
- Interact with a case study and create new understandings for attainment of Standard 4

Part 1: Examining Standard 4

The Changing View of Collaboration

Demonstrating Standard 4 within a portfolio requires an understanding of the depth and breadth of relationships. This includes recognizing relationships and learning to utilize the resources and skills that these relationships bring to the table. Collaboration is the foundation that taps into the richness that can be gleaned from utilization of these relationships.

Collaborations are organizational and interorganizational structures in which resources, power, and authority are shared, and where people are brought together to achieve common goals that could not be accomplished by a single individual or organization independently (Hosley, Gensheimer, & Yang, 2003, p. 157).

Education has a rich history of collaboration with families and communities; however, collaborations with government and private agencies are a fairly new phenomenon because it rarely occurred until the 20th century (Bray, 2003). Within this chapter, a historical overview, the current theory, and a future orientation are provided for understanding the reciprocal and dynamic relationship of collaboration in the areas of families, community, resources/partnerships, and communication. As in all best practice models of leadership, diversity will be thoughtfully and intentionally woven into the discussions for Chapter 4.

Families

Throughout the history of educational systems, parents have been involved with the education of their children. Previously, a stay-at-home parent gave administrators an established support system (Larson & Ovando, 2001). The vehicle of parent/teacher organizations was the gateway into the schools. Stay-at-home parents were quite able to form relationships with the teachers, principals, and each other. However, because of economic and social shifts, including the composition and definition of a family, the number of stay-at-home parents is on the decline, creating access challenges for parent and family involvement. Today, parent participation in their children's education is very different than it has been in past decades—an issue of access that must be addressed.

Within any school community, there are parents who are active and take leadership roles within the schools. This same school community will have parents who seek more limited opportunities to become involved, parents who want no involvement. Effective leaders recognize the differing levels of parent participation, but remain committed to access for all parents, creating capacities for all parents to participate. A caveat, however, must be issued to all future leaders: Families are composed of and defined by many different types of relationships. A single mother raising children is a family, as is two gay men raising their adopted children. The definition of family may even include a group of caregivers or grandparents raising grandchildren. As leaders within the school communities, it is not within the province of sound leadership to judge, but it is within the leadership province to respect and to model tolerance toward all families and to facilitate all families in entering a relationship with the schools. Thus, the community itself is strengthened.

The Decline of Automatic Authority

Historically, administrators want to believe the parental role is to support rules, policies, and actions of the school. However, this is no longer the norm. The era of blind agreement with school leaders is over. Decisions made solely by the once-recognized authority, the principal, will be questioned and challenged with immediacy. It now takes all the participants, particularly families, to create and maintain a successful school culture. Using a Vygotskian point of view, school cultures are socially constructed. There are social, cultural, and personal histories that are now brought into the schools. Failure on a leader's part to recognize, transform, and utilize these funds of knowledge (i.e., gifts and talents gained over the years to enrich the classroom, school, and district) will result in a weak and unsuccessful school.

Taking this point of view, it is extremely important for school leaders to invite families to school, and simply to ask about wants and needs. This means *all* families, not just the parent/teacher organization members. *All* parents need to be actively involved in the learning that is happening in the building. Effective leaders allow the parents to use their funds of knowledge—that is, the skills they have developed over the years in their personal and professional lives—to enrich the classroom and the school. How can this type of enrichment be useful? The twenty-first century holds no economic guarantee for anyone or any family (Wink & Putney, 2002). Students will need to be well rounded and exposed to many bases of knowledge. Basic skills are not going to provide enough of an educational edge for the future. The need for authentic learning is growing. "Education provides new 'tools of the intellect,' to be sure. But without contexts of use, these tools appear to 'rust'" (Cole, 1996, p. 147). For hundreds of years, schools have been a social process.

Using Parent Resources

The concept of funds of knowledge, as identified by Moll (2000), refers to "bodies of knowledge that underlie household activities" (p. 258). These are resources found in every family that school leaders can use to enrich student learning and to strengthen school/family relationships. Parents must be involved in teaching, learning, and decision making (Sergiovanni, 2001). This ultimate collaboration with families is at the foundation of the reciprocal relationship necessary for problem solving within the school community. Leaders and families engaging in activities together by sharing authentic experiences can initiate recognizing and utilizing funds of knowledge. For example, does the school need a safe playground? An effective leader will ask the parents what "funds of knowledge" (skills) they might share to create the vision of a safe playground. Can a parent who does carpentry work at home come to school and teach the children how to design the playground? The context of the playground would allow a parent/carpenter to teach the children authentic mathematics, physics, and budgeting. Not only will the real world of the students emerge, but this sharing is a way to bring diverse families together safely into the school community.

Additionally, school leaders now realize that within family and parental relationships, there exist two types of paradigms: the We-Are-Going-to-Do-This-to-You Model and the We-Are-Going-to-Do-This-with-You Model (Wink & Putney, 2002). When leaders listen and families talk, when the goal is to change the school and not the parents, when families share cultural histories and leaders do not recite meaningless objectives, a school becomes dynamic and functional (i.e., the with-You Model). However, when leaders talk and families listen, when the goal is to change the parents and guard (at all costs) the status quo of the school, when leaders promote a laundry list of meaningless objectives and families sit in silence, a school becomes static and dysfunctional—the to-You Model. Leaders cannot ask parents and families to change to meet the needs of the school. A very simple way of discovering which paradigm is in place is to observe parents at the conclusion of any parent/teacher gathering and ask the question, are the parents running out the door because they just can't get out of the building fast enough, or are the parents hanging around and talking with each other and school personnel? Another suggestion might be to ask the parents, not the teachers, if they thought the meeting was successful. Families who are members of racial and ethnic communities have very unique perceptions that need to be heard. When a group of African-American parents was asked by leaders in one study, for example, what they actually thought about their children's education and their perception of the school staff, the response was very different than leaders would have imagined:

> Many parents expressed frustration with the lack of experience that the school system's predominately White teachers seemed to have regarding the social, cultural, and often economic differences between themselves (teachers) and the students and families. (Zionts, Zionts, Harrison, & Bellinger, 2003, p. 41)

The answers will reflect either the function or the dysfunction of the building and its leadership in collaboration.

Communities

Historically, school leaders were products of their school community (i.e., a community of individuals) who, for the most part, were immersed in their personal white, European cultural backgrounds; social norms; moral values; and political agendas. Conformity reigned. This is what the leaders knew, so this is how they led. This notion of a singular purpose and attitude, however, is a notion of the past. The term *school community* now holds a much different meaning; it is no longer a singular institution with a singular purpose and mission. The school community is actually a heterogeneous sociocultural mix composed of many smaller homogeneous communities that do not hold to the white, European philosophy (Figure 4.1).

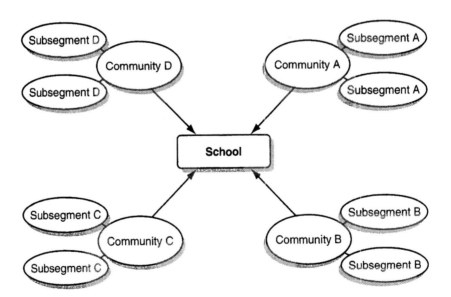

FIGURE 4.1   The School Community The school community is actually a mix of many homogeneous communities that are also composed of many subsegments. All these exert force on the school curricula and affect student learning.

Each of these homogeneous school communities insulates itself by promoting their particular cultures, norms, values, and agendas. "From birth, children interact with adults, who socialize them into their culture: their stock of meanings, their language, their conventions, and their way of doing things" (Blanck, 1984, p. 46, Figure 4.2).

The definition of community has become so diverse that there are now definitions for community, such as geographic, ethnic and racial groups, religious groups, communities based on shared family concerns, communities based on shared philanthropy, and so on (Bray, 2003).

Herein lies the challenge for leaders: the huge window for conflict and mistrust of the school by the members of the homogeneous groups. US schools and American education were not designed to support the needs of diverse, homogeneous communities with a school's environment. Any marginalized or oppressed homogeneous community that is silent or reticent to participate in the school community may be perceived by some leaders as being disinterested, resistant, and/or confrontational. This is actually an anti-institutional, yet procommunity stance. However, leaders who are insightful and intentional can resist this perceptual pitfall by recognizing and understanding that this behavior is a hallmark characteristic of years of distrust. An insightful and intentional leader can become a "socially critical leader" (Larson & Ovando, 2001). This type of leader can begin ameliorating

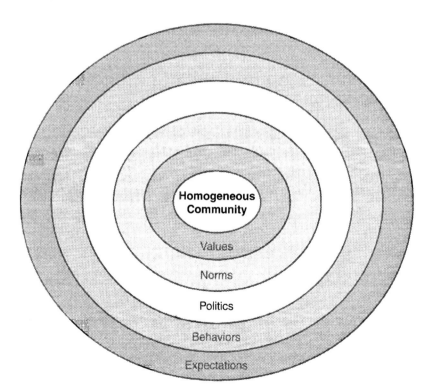

FIGURE 4.2   The Homogeneous Community Each homogeneous community is insulated by the history of its culture.

the distrust and begin collaborating immediately through recognition and understanding. This attitude initiates community-inclusive leadership. Leaders who recognize communities and build trust create "social capital" (Print & Coleman, 2003). Social capital can readily improve the school community by a joint effort toward reaching learning goals.

Understanding the Numerous Communities

Leaders next must be cognizant that every child in the building is a member of a homogeneous community. The school community is perceived as wrought with barriers and, in some cases, is an unwelcoming and unsafe environment. A leader's understanding of each homogeneous community in the school can soften this perception and open lines of access for collaborative activities. It is these collaborative activities involving all the homogeneous communities within the school that can be a significant force in student learning, positive change, improvements, and access. Furthermore,

> Community knowledge is a valuable commodity in any classroom, but is especially important in communities serving multiracial and multiethnic populations because greater connections with communities can help to bridge the gap existing between the lives and experiences of educators and their students. (Larson & Ovando, 2001, p. 196)

This approach is of particular importance for the homogeneous communities within a school that are economically vulnerable. Poverty's most overwhelming and pervasive symptoms are chaos and violence. Yet, many school leaders fail to recognize this:

> The havoc that poverty wreaks in children's lives and in the lives and life opportunities of their families often goes unrecognized and misunderstood by many educators. Educators often misunderstand why children are late or absent, improperly dressed, or unprepared. Grounded in the privilege of their own lives, educators often believe that these behaviors indicate uncaring parents and undisciplined children. (Larson & Ovando, 2001, p. 190)

Leaders who fail to realize these effects are immersed in the bureaucratic methods and attitudes of closed systems of control. This method is no longer working in schools. Leaders cannot continue to perceive themselves as the sole experts in education. The community has a democratic right and an ethical right to participate in school decision making. If leaders allow the community into the process, they are resisting this closed system that is now failing schools. It takes a courageous leader to resist the current system. Most leaders do not possess this courage, and are still under the dangerously false impression that control will only increase the conflict between the school and the various diverse and homogeneous communities that create the school community. However, it is the closed system that "actually perpetuate[s] many of the conflicts we encounter in schools today" (Larson & Ovando, 2001, p. 169). And ignoring or burying conflict does not work in a school either. Ask any seasoned administrator if it solves the problem, and the response will most likely be: The problem will come back threefold at the most inopportune time. This is the nature of the beast. Even the poster child action of a closed system, expulsion, is both ineffective and only promotes one of the most deplorable attitudes of American society:

Young people are disposable, right along with trash. It's an easy, clean method of problem solving. Yet, it is ineffective. It solves nothing. What, then, can leaders do?

Leaders can open doors and stop both exclusion and segregation. They can intentionally invite all members of the school community into the decision-making process. Leaders can begin listening to their community members, particularly the critics. As ridiculously simple as this sounds, from these inside collaborations, leaders can learn and grow. When leaders learn and grow, so do their schools and students.

Resources and Partnerships

Aside from families and communities who are directly involved with the schools, leaders also need to look to other resources and partnerships to broaden the scope of collaboration. When thinking of external collaborations, leaders first need to understand that a school within any community is both a building and an institution. As buildings, the facilities can be used for many community activities and organizational meetings after hours. As institutions, they can be at the forefront of many educational programs within the community. However, the overall goal should be to better the children's opportunities for success as learners and citizens.

When establishing resources and partnerships for a stronger learning community, Change Agentry Theory can be very useful because it can guide leaders in the development of collaborative relationships that will change for the better both the school and the agencies and organizations with which the school is collaborating (Fullan, 1993). The collaboration process will change both the school and the agency or organization (Green, 2001). School leaders need to consider this first and foremost. To build a relationship, leaders should realize the four core capacities that can be applied to building relationships with agencies and organizations by improving curricular offerings, diminishing duplication of offerings, and bolstering offerings:

1. *Shared vision:* A collective purpose needs to be shared by all stakeholders.
2. *Inquiry:* A continual assessment needs to be in place.
3. *Mastery:* New ideas and skills are understood and accepted.
4. *Collaboration:* Both the school and the agency/organization have the appropriate attitudes and willingness to share abilities (Fullan, 1993).

There are many areas for leaders looking for resources and partnership to explore to strengthen the learning mission of the schools. Again, these collaborations can enhance any school's curriculum:

- *Community collaborations:* This can occur between other institutions/organizations/agencies supported by local tax dollars or privately funded agencies. These would include community education programs, health services, and libraries.
- *Business collaborations:* These give students authentic opportunities to use their learning in the real world and to explore the realities of probable career choices. For teachers, being hired for summer employment benefits both parties and, in particular, the students benefit from the authentic learning of the teachers.

- *University collaborations:* Colleges of education wrestle with similar issues as those in elementary and secondary education. Collaborations can range from meeting student needs (advanced coursework and counseling), professional development, action research, grants, joint practices, mentoring, and team teaching (Danielson, 2002).

When beginning a collaborative activity with these outside agencies and organizations, leaders need to state very clearly and stress the benefits of the relationships with the schools for agencies and organizations. Given the current state of economics, when these institutions may be fierce competitors with each other and see the school as a major competitor for funding, the emphasis on the benefits of partnership cannot be overstated. One such benefit can be the sharing of activities, responsibilities, and personnel to reach particular goals. For some agencies and organizations, school families and/or parents may be prospective clients who will in turn become paying customers for services. Some students may even opt to work or to volunteer within the agencies and organizations after graduation. The most significant benefit for the schools, the community, the agencies, and the organizations, however, will be the demonstration and support for lifelong learning for everyone.

A foundational issue that needs to be addressed when collaborating with any segment of the community is trust. This is a particularly sensitive issue within minority communities. With majority communities—that is, communities that share educators' and leaders' social and racial backgrounds—trust is not an issue (Larson & Ovando, 2001). However, contact can bridge the trust issue. Through the simple acts of initiating contact, listening, and understanding, trust can be built. "One of the greatest obstacles to establishing more trusting and equitable relationships with the multiple communities we serve is accepting that our perceptions of others are susceptible to misperception and bias" (Larson & Ovando, 2001, p. 64). Unfortunately, many leaders become blind to the differences in communities, and therefore they become blind to the needs and the possibilities. Some leaders immerse themselves in universalism: Communities are all the same. Yes, some sameness exists, but there are also some compelling differences that can enrich learning in the building. The blindness itself is presumptive and exclusionary in nature. Neutrality is not the answer for trust within the homogeneous communities that create the school community.

Communication

School leaders will spend up to 80 percent of their work time involved in communications with those in and outside the school (Sobel & Ornstein, 1996). "Therefore, tantamount to the school operating in an efficient and effective manner is the leader's ability to communicate with people" (Green, 2001). Communication is foundational in forming relationships outside the school. Therefore, communication with all sectors should be planned and proactive, not reactive. Leaders have enough obstacles in creating collaborations; they don't need to undermine themselves. Historically, there are three arenas of communication to glean collaborations for a school: individual families, the school community itself, and the public at large. These are all school clients. Communicating with these groups takes the forms of shared decision making (e.g., intentional dialogue), parent community support (e.g., economic support), and public relations (e.g., information). All these support the culture of learning with the school and help the school to be perceived as a center for learning (Danielson, 2002). Leaders who use all these arenas develop successful and effective communication lines, and do get support for the children and the school as an institution. This use of intentional dialogue opens the school to families and to the community. Conversations begin to take place about the purposes and practices of the school. The purposes and practices of the school are then understood, and the barrier of inequity is diminished (Larson & Ovando, 2001). The more community members and communities are sought out and intentionally invited to the schools, the greater the educational and economic support.

Within schools, there are some barriers that have been identified that will limit effective communication of leaders:

1. *Information overload:* So much information is generated and disseminated that the receiver could not possibly read it all or digest any of it.
2. *Status difference:* Open, two-way communication is diminished because of a difference in the power of status (e.g., a parent of a student with a behavioral disorder is hesitant to send an e-mail message to the principal).
3. *Semantics:* Words have different meanings for those of different races and cultures. For example, "that's bad" would carry the meaning of "that's good" within the African-American community, but would mean "that's not good" in the white Anglo community.
4. *Filtering:* The original communication from the sender is altered, either intentionally or unintentionally, or only a part of the original is sent or received.
5. *Paralanguage:* Body language, patter (speed and cadence), and emotional intonations (sighs, grunts) are used in spoken language.
6. *Interpersonal relationships:* The quality and interpersonal styles of the participants in the communication are important (Green, 2001).

Effective leaders must always assume that there will be obstacles in any communication, and the receiver of the message may not interpret the message as expected. It is sound practice to let a few other professionals read the message, particularly those that are sensitive or highly important, before the sending the message on to the receivers. The feedback should be taken seriously, and changes made if necessary. Also, look at the message and determine whether any repercussions can be anticipated.

Leaders must be concerned with their utterances. Speech is an activity that carries with each word a historical, institutional, cultural, and individual meaning. One's voice can reveal a speaker's subjective emotional evaluation of a situation. Social speech type refers to the perspective or point of view to be taken. Lastly, dialogue should also be given some thought. Speech causes reactions and may cause anticipation for future reactions. When attempting collaborative activities, leaders must pay close attention to the sociocultural context.

Again, there is a caveat: It must be emphasized that when communication is stopped, is shut down, or is only one-way, confrontation will more than likely occur. Stopping conversation does not stop the problem; it simply incubates the issue so it can fester and grow. Ending communication will end collaborations. Once ended, it is difficult (if not impossible) to regain the trust in collaborations.

Some of the most effective strategies that can be used to remove barriers and improve the quality of communication are

- Establishing effective interpersonal relationships
- Managing position power (i.e., power associated with a position such as principal)
- Acquiring feedback
- Displaying empathy (Green, 2001, p. 103)

The benefits of breaking down the barriers will be foundational for forming, nurturing, and saving collaborative relationships.

Families

Currently, too many schools have a closed system of communicating with families. This is fine for simply disseminating general information. However, this is a serious issue considering active parental involvement is a significant factor in student success and decision making (Ovando & Collier, 1998). The majority of parents are not interested in the minutiae of their children's performances; rather, they are only interested in knowing their children are on track (Danielson, 2002). For student success, there must be established one-way and two-way streets for communication, and communication to the school must be invited and welcomed. This communication must also be varied for an effective school (Sergiovanni, 2001). Parents need to visit the schools, but they are more often than not reluctant to do so, and are certainly reluctant to make the first move toward collaboration (Bagin & Gallagher, 2001). This model goes well beyond the two most common reasons for a leader to communicate with a parent: a serious behavior problem or needed classroom help. Once families hear that there is an open-door policy in the school, usually through mass media and parents who have already taken advantage of the policy, they become curious and make the move to take advantage of the policy (Bagin & Gallagher, 2001). Leaders also need to make certain that they are not exclusionary when it comes to low socioeconomic status families or poverty-level families. These families care just as much about their children as upper socioeconomic families. Economic situations do not dictate the level of parental concern.

School leaders realize that most communication with families comes from teachers. However, it is up to the leaders to encourage communication that is two-way, open, and active, and that schoolwide communication supplements the individual teachers' methods with schoolwide lines of communication. These schoolwide lines of communication must also be two-way, open, and active to be effective. If there are non-English speaking families, ESL (English as a second language) families, or LEP (limited English proficiency) families in the school community, communication should be in the families' first languages. Many leaders have sought out ethnic media specialists to help communicate accurately with these groups (Bagin & Gallagher, 2001). It is also necessary for school leaders to let teachers know they are willing to work with the teachers on their individual communications with parents to make certain that notes and letters sent home are culturally sensitive and contain no insults based on socioeconomic status. For instance, consider the note sent home to a family that is led by caregivers, rather than parents, and is addressed to

"Mom and Dad." Or, consider the permission slip sent home to a lower socioeconomic family asking them on Monday "to donate $25 by Friday for a field trip." It is the leader's responsibility to nurture awareness in their staff.

Leaders must also be exceptionally careful that school personnel do not depend on technology as a vehicle of communication. Within many low socioeconomic and poverty—level family homes, computers are not available, even though computer terminals my be quite plentiful within the schools. Therefore, posting information on a website, for example, may be useless for some families.

The School Community

The school community often falls prey to overuse of the one-way system of communication. The one-way system does need to be in place for disseminating general information, because communities care about what is happening in the schools. The more communities know about the school, the more support the school will receive. However, the need for a two-way process is evident in collaborative activities, such as learning. The more schools open themselves to the communities with two-way communication opportunities, the more responsive the community will become. "Through effective communication, relationships are built, trust is established, and respect is gained" (Green, 2001, p. 95). School leaders need to remember that for most communities, schools are not a comfortable place to be. The school culture and behavioral norms may be very different from their own culture and behavioral norms, which will cause fear of the unknown. This fear is very real, and the more dichotomous the school culture is from the particular homogeneous culture of the community, the more fearful community members will be. Thus, it is the process of communication that can ameliorate the fear and bridge the cultures.

Before beginning any collaborative activity within the school community, there must be certain knowledges in place for the leaders. Leaders must first know and understand the power structure, the process for decision making, the media workings, the expectations of the community, the groups that will help the school, the groups that will initiate confrontations for any reason, and the channels of public opinion (Bagin & Gallagher, 2001). Only then should collaboration begin.

If school leaders emphasize the importance of culturally sensitive communication, limit the amount of mass communication and form letters, and encourage communication that is written specifically for particular segments or particular homogeneous communities within the school community, the school doors will be perceived as open and willing to field the needs of the communities. Insensitive communications will only further a sense of fear, and sometimes even resentment. The school will be perceived as an unwelcoming, uncaring place. The exclusionary approach will only feed the tensions that already exist in every community. When fear is removed, creativity is enhanced and stimulated. A foundation and capacity for change is developed. This leads to more productivity in the collaborative relationship. Once school leaders develop a two-way process that is sensitive to the fear of the unknown, many benefits will arise. Some of these benefits include the identification of authentic weaknesses and strengths, financial support, philanthropic support, and help in decision making.

There is a current theory that people within the school community will not accept or will reject ideas for change or reform until they have spoken with other community members who are perceived as "key communicators" (Bagin & Gallagher, 2001). Because key communicators are very much people persons, they more than likely have the power not only to communicate the pulse of the community in a single phone call, but also have the power to stop rumors. A key communicator is not only a sound orator, but is also someone who has a sound rapport with school leaders and can communicate confidence and trust to the rest of the community. Once a leader identifies this person, this is a tremendous advantage in getting the public positively involved in the school. Because the community trusts the key communicator, confidence and trust are transferred back to the community. If a key communicator cannot be immediately identified, then the leader should undertake a purposeful search for one (Bagin & Gallagher, 2001). Leaders can ask their staff for assistance in suggesting some names. Once some possible communicators have been identified, they may be sent invitations to serve in this position. It has been found that if the superintendent of schools sends the invitation, the response will be very high (Bagin & Gallagher, 2001). The superintendent may then invite all to meet at a very informal lunch or dinner. This should be an open-ended confidence-building session that should be held at least once a year.

The Public at Large

When working with the public at large in collaborative activities, there are three areas of communication in which a leader must become proficient. The first area is a leader's ability to rally others in the pursuit of like goals. Leaders must be able to influence the public to value their goals and to help them to reach those goals. Therefore, in communication, leaders need to project a sense of enthusiasm and confidence. Relationships must be the second concern for leaders in the communication process. The establishment of sound relationships must be made. Leaders should pay close attention to communicating trust and personal commitment to a collaboration. The third area is predicated upon a leader's ability to listen and hear the information the public finds important and necessary. It is this part that empowers the public within a collaborative relationship and equals the playing field (i.e., puts forth the notion that everyone, and everyone's ideas, are important in the relationship). Hearing from greater numbers of more diverse communities only increases the chance of success. A leader who does not hear and listen will risk never having any collaborative relationship with the public.

Just like within a community, leaders must understand the power structure, the communication patterns, channels of public opinion, and the process of decision making within the public realm. The media needs to be analyzed right along with the expectations of the citizenry. Friendly groups need to be identified as well as those that are unwilling to collaborate with the school. All of this is important groundwork before the approach (Bagin & Gallagher, 2001).

Taking this one step further, leaders who do not go into the many diverse homogeneous communities that make up the school community itself risk stereotyping and making assumptions in their communications that they would not have made if they had simply taken their messages into the racial, ethnic, and lower socioeconomic segments they serve. This would diminish the naive misunderstandings and problematic images that members of the leadership may hold, and then—either intentionally or unintentionally—communicate publicly. Knowing where children and parents in a community live and how they live is the first step in communicating a sincere interest and concern for the school population (Larson & Ovando, 2001). For instance, a school can be a very different place for a white student, a black student, a Latino student, a student from a rich family, and a student from a poor family. Leaders need to realize and communicate this knowledge accurately and sensitively.

One area that many school leaders can easily develop for the initiation of collaborative relationships within the public realm is students themselves: their activities, publications, and productions. When the public enjoys any of these activities, the opinions within the community are positive and the ground is fertile for beginning collaborations. Examples of these activities include public presentations, musical programs, dramatic productions, special assemblies, field trips, athletics, commencement, work–study programs, and awards banquets and programs (Bagin & Gallagher, 2001). However, all and any of these programs need a curricular link—that is, the program itself needs clearly to be a part of the learning in the building. This learning link also needs to be either articulated during the program by the school leader or identified in writing within the program brochure/booklet.

Public Relations

Public relations itself may be perceived by school leaders as a complicated management issue. Before going into the "how to's" of public relations, it is first important to understand a definition of public relations: "Public relations is the management function which evaluates public attitudes, identifies the policies and procedures of an individual or an organization with the public interest, and plans and executes a program of action to earn public understanding and acceptance" (Griswold, 1992, p. 7). Within schools, public relations are all the above, with emphasis on improving school programs and services within a two-way path of communication (National School Public Relations Association, 1985). However, if leaders put into place a public relations program within the framework of student achievement and public support, the complexities will fade. Programs should be designed to encourage the following:

- Promote a positive and challenging school climate in which student achievement and staff productivity are fostered
- Encourage maximum involvement of parents, at home and in school, in their children's educational development
- Involve citizens in cooperative learning practices, partnerships, and other learning resources in the community
- Build public knowledge of the purposes, successes, and needs of the school system, leading to public understanding and support (Bagin & Gallagher, 2001, p. 7)

Student achievement demands both a positive and safe learning environment, family and public involvement, and the public knowledge and support that underpin financial support. However, communication with the public is sometimes challenging for school leaders. A former public relations director for the Pennsylvania State Education Department identified the reasons some school leaders are very poor communicators. These reasons warrant a serious look by all school leaders, no matter how well they think they can communicate with the public sector. The pitfalls for educators are the following:

- They have a false impression about their ability to communicate. Communication involves disseminating information, getting a response, and evaluating that response.
- Educators aren't used to competing for people's attention. They have enjoyed the luxury of waiting for the public to come to them.
- Many educators operated in relative obscurity for many years and are unprepared for the public's accelerating interest in their activities. They consider the scrutinizing of their activities to be inappropriate.
- Educators have such a high regard for their colleagues' professional ability that they unconsciously minimize the value of outside opinion.
- Most professional educators—especially those in administrative positions—have little communication experience and almost no meaningful communication training. (Holliday, 1988, p. 12)

Avoiding these pitfalls will bring about an increased use of school resources by an appreciative public, increased support from the public, and a total integration of school–community relationships.

There is always a gray zone in working directly with the media. Although reporters have a right to know, just how much must a school leader disclose and what do the reporters have a right to know? In addition to supporting a plan that proactively shares school and district news, it is suggested that school leaders consider these suggestions:

- Answer all questions honestly, and respond promptly to reporters' deadlines.
- Remember that all reports and surveys belong to the public and, as such, are public property.
- Release information in a timely fashion.
- Don't use educational jargon.
- Use approximate figures; it's fine to do so.
- Don't hesitate to say, "I don't know."
- Be as accurate as possible.
- Understand how risky "off the record" is in reality.
- Talk with reporters on a first-name basis.
- Let supervisors know immediately after talking to the press about an important issue.
- Have a directory of key media contacts.
- Be available for negative news too.
- Give home phone numbers to the media so rumors can be immediately squelched and accurate facts given (Bagin & Gallagher, 2001).

Part 2: Key Performances, Knowledges, and Dispositions for Standard 4

Key Performances

The beginning of this chapter gave a social, cultural, and historical context for understanding, finding, and utilizing the funds of knowledge and resources available within each school community. Now, in this part, the theories of collaboration are authenticated by relating them to the everyday practices of school leaders.

The key elements of this standard are collaborating with families and community members, responding to diverse communities, and mobilizing community resources. These elements will be discussed in Part 2, along with supporting their importance in leadership. As the Reverend Dr. Martin Luther King, Jr., once so eloquently stated, "We are caught in an inescapable network of mutuality, tied in a single garment of destiny. Whatever affects one directly, affects all indirectly" (as cited in Lacey, 2005, p. 1).

Performances
The administrator facilitates processes and engages in activities ensuring that

1. High visibility, active involvement, and communication with the larger community occurs
2. Relationships with community leaders are established and nurtured
3. Respect is given to individuals and groups whose values, opinions, and cultures may conflict
4. Information about family and community concerns, expectations, and needs is used regularly
5. There is outreach to different business, religious, political, and service agencies and organizations
6. The school and community serve one another as resources
7. Available community resources are secured to help the school solve problems and goals
8. Partnerships are established with area businesses, institutions of higher education, and community groups to strengthen programs and support school goals
9. Community stakeholders are treated equitably
10. Effective media relations are developed and maintained
11. A comprehensive program of community relations is established
12. Public resources and funds are used appropriately and wisely
13. Community collaborations are modeled for staff
14. Opportunities for staff to develop collaborative skills are provided
15. Multicultural awareness, gender sensitivity, and racial and ethnic appreciation are promoted

In these 15 performances, family and community take precedence. It is these two groups to which the school has a direct responsibility, and with which they share a reciprocal relationship in the educational success of the children. Some basic knowledge on how to build these relationships/collaborations can be gleaned from a group that has many ties with schools: the American Speech–Language–Hearing Association. Before contacting any community group or family, they recommend that, if the group or family is a different culture than the leader's group or family, to become as knowledgeable as possible about the community's and family's interests, history, customs, and particularly the style of interactions (Huer & Saenz, 2003). They also warn that even knowing all of the preceding information, it is still necessary to remember that there are wide variations in every community and family (Huer & Saenz, 2003). School leaders can also take a lesson from a public leader in community collaborations—the Public Health Systems Research Affiliate of the Academy for Health Services Research and Health Policy. Before collaborations within any community take place, the leaders gather information and evidence in the following areas for each community or agency:

- Current organization and operation
- Scope and scale of services
- Effectiveness and efficiency of organizational and financial characteristics
- Overall performance effectiveness (Mays, Halverson, & Scutchfield, 2003).

As discussed in Part 1, a child's education is very much dependent on the family's support and interest. The school does not act alone, and strong leaders will, for the sake of the child, actively and intentionally seek out the families' help and input in decision making concerning the child. It is the family that knows the child best, and how the child behaves and learns in an authentic environment.

If leaders serve the community well, by both sharing information and listening to the wants and needs of its members, the community will be very giving to the school and the children in the school. Community members will even enrich the classroom with their funds of knowledge. For instance, many schools that have had problems with violence have taken the police and security guards out of the schools and replaced them with parents and concerned members of the community. They got this idea from the Africans who use "overmothering" within their institutions. Parents and people within the community care about the students in the school. Through this caring by supportive adults, violence has been eradicated. Obviously, not all the support from family and community needs to be of an economic nature. There is a richness that can transcend all aspects of the school, if the leader is open to the support, and communicates this to the families and communities.

A large part of this sharing and listening involves strategies for initial steps in learning about the communities that comprise the school (Soto, Huer, & Taylor, 1997). At the top of the list are informal conversations with community members. Also, simply observing individuals from different cultural backgrounds within their own environment, where typical interactions take place, is very helpful. A leader may wish to patronize several local businesses to interact in multiple environments. Social activities are another source to gain insight into the realities and informal communication patterns of a community. Leaders may wish to attend a local Serbian fest or a general prayer meeting in a mosque, for example. Another strategy for a school leader is to seek out the local university for assistance.

Having informal conversations with graduate students may be a very helpful resource because these students are usually quite knowledgeable about their own cultural communities. These types of informal conversation are extremely beneficial for dispositional knowledge and informal background on the perception of the community toward the school.

There are various websites that leaders can look to for ideas on learning partnerships within communities. At *www.cde.ca.gov/ls/pf/co/*, ideas for after-school education, international education, and health education can be obtained. This site also offers a plethora of printed resources for leaders who are interested in casting a wider net for resources within communities. Also, a guide to developing educational partnerships can be downloaded from *http://www.ed.gov/about/offices/list/oiia/oia.html*. This very thorough examination helps leaders by giving them very practical ideas to initiate and nurture partnerships, and to sustain partnership activities. There are ideas from practicing and ongoing partnerships. Another part of this website contains the article "Educational Partnerships Case Studies," which is valuable for leaders who wish to create partnerships to help with changes in the school. Furthermore, the section on "Conducting Needs Assessments: Practices That Support Partnership Building" gives leaders tips on how to facilitate this process, and case studies from successful programs. Recognizing that partnerships depend on community and family involvement, there is also a detailed section on community involvement. Again, a strong and practical portion is dedicated to the "how to," and several best practice cases are detailed.

Representative Comments Demonstrating Emerging Performances for Standard 4

- At a faculty meeting the principal announces: "I am volunteering at the YMCA and giving presentations on parent–child relationships. What are some ways you think you might interact with the community to enhance our school's collaboration with them? What are your special talents? Let's find ways that we can all work with the community in ways that celebrate our strengths."
- At a PTO meeting the principal announces: "Let's develop a schoolwide initiative to celebrate the diverse cultures we have in our community and school. Where might we begin?"
- "How can I sustain and nurture my relationship with the Citizens for Community Action Coalition?"

Representative Actions Demonstrating Emerging Performances for Standard 4

- The principal joins the Lions Club and other civic organizations in the community.
- The principal forms a diversity task force made up of teachers, parents, and community leaders who represent various ethnicities in the community.
- The principal seeks out and applies for state, federal, and foundation-based grants that assist schools in recognizing and celebrating diversity in the school and community.
- The principal contacts the local TV, radio station, and newspaper to inform them of the special program the students are presenting on African-American culture and invites them to attend.

Key Knowledges and Dispositions

Previously this chapter demonstrated how an effective administrator will use the performances associated with Standard 4 to develop a management pedagogy. In addition to performances, Standard 4 contains knowledges and dispositions. This section will assist the administrator in building behaviors that demonstrate attainment of the knowledges and dispositions. The following lists detail the key knowledges and dispositions from Standard 4:

Knowledges
The administrator has a knowledge and understanding of

1. Emerging issues and trends that potentially impact the school community
2. The conditions and dynamics of the diverse school community
3. Community resources
4. Community relations and marketing strategies and processes
5. Successful models of school, family, business, community, government, and higher education partnerships
6. Community and district power structures

Dispositions
The administrator believes in, values, and is committed to

1. Schools operating as an integral part of the larger community
2. Collaboration and communication with families and community
3. Involvement of families and other stakeholders in school decision-making processes
4. The proposition that diversity can enrich the school
5. Families as partners in the education of their children
6. Using community resources to enhance the education of students
7. Informing the public
8. Schools and families keeping the best interests of children in mind

Key Knowledges

The building of relationships with all stakeholders is embedded in the six knowledges. It is critical, then, for sound leaders to do their homework before even attempting to initiate any relationship. The leader must do some informal research and gather the oral history of families and communities before making any attempt at collaboration. There is no substitute for this proaction. Reaction risks failure. It is also very important not to limit collaboration to those groups within the school. A leader must be willing to go out into the public and exhaust the possibilities of collaborative opportunities. The more support a leader can gather, the more support the children receive and the better their educational opportunities. Leaders must approach all communities that compose the school community in an unbiased manner. Everyone has the capacity to make a genuine contribution.

Currently, there is a particular need to establish these outside links for educational and economic reasons: Duplicating services within any community is now becoming extremely costly, given the lack of funding to education from the states. Any time leaders can collaborate with an agency, private or government, to serve the children of their schools, teaching and learning benefits. In particular, there has been a recent sharp increase in university/school collaborations (Ansari, 2003). For instance, Michigan State University has been successful in teaming with schools on curricula decisions. East Tennessee State University has helped schools with ferreting out community needs and then tweaking curricula to meet those needs. Globally, examples can be found in South African universities that have helped schools to redesign curricula to increase access for community participation. The university–school relationship is one leaders should not ignore. Not only can universities help in the obvious ways involving curricula and professional development, but these collaborations can also be developed to generate the behind-the-scenes information necessary for relationships, including cultural information, needs assessments, and so forth. Furthermore, partnering can serve as an excellent recruitment tool for universities, providing rich opportunities to develop a new cadre of teachers.

Representative Comments Demonstrating Emerging Knowledges for Standard 4

- "What are we going to do about the pending retirement of five teachers in my school? Are there 'highly qualified' teachers available to take their positions?"
- "How are the state budget cuts and local property tax referendum going to impact the district and school? How might we garner the support of the community to increase the property tax rate?"

Representative Actions Demonstrating Emerging Knowledges for Standard 4

- The principal initiates a book club, providing teachers with books that are based on various best practice models. A voluntary weekly discussion of the book and its implications for classroom practice is conducted after school.
- A professionally printed brochure with a picture of the school, a staff picture, the mission and vision statements, and a summary of school goals and accomplishments is developed by a team of teachers, students, and parents, and is distributed throughout the community.

Key Dispositions

Leaders who want a strong institution need to welcome disagreements and challenges. This is how an institution will grow in a positive and meaningful manner. These eight standards confirm this. It is through this positive tension that the curriculum and process of education meet the needs of the students, and keep quality within the curriculum. The more diversity of thought and ideas that can be generated and examined before a decision is made, the better the decision will be for the students. Conformity is no longer the goal of education for leaders. Every administrative act should have one goal: to better the education of all students. The posturing and the attitude of leaders should relay this to all within their communities. Student welfare should drive each and every plan, action, and decision.

Cross-cultural collaborations have a strong dispositional component, as witnessed in this set of standards. The Amherst H. Wilder Foundation's Social Adjustment Program for Southeast Asians is an example of a school program that is sensitive to the dispositional aspect of communities and families. They found that building cross-cultural collaborations is difficult, particularly if the school and the communities have not had occasion to work together. From their challenges, however, school leaders can benefit. If language differences exist, the leaders should always attempt to conduct the initial meetings in the community's first language, not the leaders' first language.

The *success* of a multicultural collaboration is directly related to trust and relationship building, which is grounded in mutual respect for differences in cultural styles. These different cultural styles and approaches should be incorporated into all aspects of the collaboration, including the structure of meetings, decision making, and communication patterns. Multicultural collaborations should provide for the full access and participation of all partners, and may include conducting meetings and events bilingually. Bilingual and bicultural staff serve as important bridges across communities (Hosley, Gensheimer, & Yang, 2003).

Initially in the Social Adjustment Program, many families tended to see the school leaders as the experts. Families were extremely hesitant to participate as partners until trust was generated. When the parents saw that the pace of meetings was slowed to accommodate their second-language fluency, interpreters were provided at each and every session so they could fully understand the discussions. Once their input was sought, invited, and taken seriously, and they had a meaningful role in the collaboration, they found that they had a voice and vote in the decision making, and a trusting relationship was built (Hosley, Gensheimer, & Yang, 2003).

Another suggestion for working with multicultural families and communities arises from research prompted by The Individuals with Disabilities Education Act (IDEA). Researchers found that as studies go forward in both complexity and quality, "generic" parental input and program characteristics are now useless (Zionts, Zionts, Harrison, & Bellinger, 2003). This only serves to reaffirm the notion that color blindness has no place in current educational environments (Larson & Ovando, 2001). "Generic" cases, wants, and needs cannot exist in a school community. Another example of this can be found from another IDEA study that, indeed, followed the advice of no generic data. Researchers found that Latino/Latina parents were less involved in their children's education; however, they were very satisfied with the education their children were receiving. They further found that African-American parents who were non-Christian felt their children were subjected to discrimination, particularly on major Christian holidays and non-Christian holidays (Zionts, Harrison, & Bellinger, 2003). Thus, both of these facts would have been barriers to collaboration if they had not been addressed by the school leader. It is important to remember that leaders, when attempting to understand communities, must take into account many things when communicating and collaborating with their students, staff, and school community, including geographical regions, ethnicity, gender, race, socioeconomic status, sexual orientation, religious affiliation, level of education, age, marital status, caregiver status, and number of children per household. Only then will they have a sound look at the community that they serve.

Representative Comments Demonstrating Emerging Dispositions for Standard 4

- "The adoption of textbooks is a time-consuming task, but we must make our choices based on what the best selection is for our student population."
- "We should ask members of the Senior Citizens Center if they would like to help with tutoring students after school in reading and math."

Representative Actions Demonstrating Emerging Dispositions for Standard 4

- The school website is designed to allow parents to ask questions and provide feedback on various school programs. To allow all parents equal access, students take home a "Questions & Comments" sheet on a monthly basis. Parents may respond online or may return the sheet to the school.
- The principal participates in a weekly radio show during which the community can call in with questions. The principal also has an opportunity at the beginning of the show to share school news and provide listeners with a specific topic for discussion (e.g., the upcoming statewide test, pointers on how to get students to do homework, etc.).

Specific steps for building the portfolio are discussed in the next section. In addition, refer to the accompanying CD-ROM for further activities related to Standard 4.

Part 3: Portfolio Exercise for Standard 4

The following exercise will help students seeking administrative licensure to build their professional portfolio. Procedures are described here that will lead to a completed entry for a professional portfolio (Standard 4). A five-level scoring rubric to measure the level of standard attainment is contained in Appendix B. The rubric provides the rater with scoring criteria to evaluate the portfolio exercise.

1. Access your file box, the Standard 4 divider, and three manila folders.
2. Think about how the theories of collaboration within each school community can be authenticated by relating them to the everyday practice of school leaders. Consider how you would promote the success of all learners by recognizing collaborative relationships and utilizing the resources and skills that these relationships bring to the table as discussed in Chapter 4. Choose an activity that would demonstrate your competence in this area. Examples include working with the Hispanic community to develop an adult literacy program targeted to parents of at-risk Hispanic students; involving the community of students, parents, and other interested parties in developing and implementing a school improvement plan; and establishing a partnership with local businesses to help provide financial support for after-school programs to remediate reading and math deficiencies of their employees and high school students. Think about the knowledges performances, and dispositions associated with Standard 4, and discuss them in your narrative section.
3. Conduct the activity you select and keep a record of how it was enacted (videotape, tape recorder, journal entries, etc.).
4. Once the activity is complete, review your video, audio, or written record and reflect on what happened and how it relates to Standard 4. The reflection should include a narrative description of what you did, who was involved, when it occurred, and the outcome. Upon reflection, what would you do differently if you had the opportunity to perform the activity again?
5. Discuss how the activity shows partial attainment of Standard 4.

6. Provide written authenticity for the activity. For example, your principal or supervisor writes a letter attesting to your performance of the activity, or a policy statement is developed or shared.
7. Place the videotape, audiotape, or electronic medium in one folder. Place the reflections and authenticity evidence in the two remaining folders.
8. Carefully review all items and correct any errors.

A sample portfolio artifact follows.

BOX **4.1**

Sample Portfolio Entry

Artifact for Standard 4: Collaboration with Families and the Community

Names of Artifacts: video of interview on *News from Our Schools* article from *Williamsport Times*

Date: June 12, 20XX

Franklin Elementary School

Williamsport School District

Artifacts

The video is of a 30-minute local cable television program, *News from Our Schools,* which is broadcast monthly during the school year. During this program, I am being interviewed about the proposed renovation and expansion of Franklin Elementary School. Three members of the committee who worked with the architects in designing the construction project join me on this program. The newspaper article highlights the recent groundbreaking ceremony for this project.

Reflection Narrative

Several years ago, the need for an expansion of Franklin Elementary School became evident. Growth in the housing market in the Franklin district was increasing every year, and our enrollment was skyrocketing. The school had been using portable classrooms for the last five years, but even they were no longer adequate for our burgeoning school population. With the help of several committed parent volunteers, I initiated a petition drive to expand and renovate our 45-year-old building. We held several public meetings at the school to showcase our overcrowding problems for the community. Following these meetings, key parent volunteers, several teachers, and I went door-to-door in the community, seeking support for the needed renovations and expansion.

Our petition drive was successful, and the school board approved funding for the project. As principal of the school, I headed the committee to work with the architects on designing the project. The existing multipurpose room was to be converted to a cafeteria. A kitchen, gymnasium, media center, art room, music room, office, and kindergarten wing were to be added to the facility. The existing media center; kindergarten rooms; office, art, and music rooms would be converted to classrooms; and the entire building would be updated for wiring and plumbing. New carpet and paint in the existing part of the building would complete the renovations. The team that worked with the architect to develop these plans included six parents, six teachers, the media specialist, the associate superintendent for business, and the food services supervisor.

The enclosed video is a recording of a 30-minute program during which I shared with the community our plans for the project. I invited three committee members to join me on this program: a teacher who could explain the academic benefits of the proposed revisions, a parent who could discuss her perceptions of the impact this project would have on the students, and our associate superintendent for business, who could address any questions about the funding for the project.

I approached the producer of this program about doing a segment on the Franklin School Renovation and Expansion Project because I felt it was important to keep the community informed about it. As I look back at the tape, I feel several important goals were accomplished. Perhaps most important, the community was able to see that the families of our students were partners throughout this process. They worked with us on the petition drive and they were part of the design team. Without the efforts of the parent association, the petition drive would most likely have failed. This program, which would be broadcast to the community eight times during a four-week period, provided an opportunity to acknowledge their contributions and thank them for their efforts. The groundbreaking ceremony offered another opportunity to acknowledge their role.

The participation of parents and teachers during the design phase of this project was crucial. The parents were able to see why the teachers felt a need for certain aspects to be included (or excluded from) the design, and the teachers became more sensitive to the concerns of the families. Throughout the process, the diversity of opinions expressed led to the development of greater understanding on everyone's part of the needs of all segments of our school community.

Scoring Analysis for the Entry
Using the portfolio exercise scoring rubric (Appendix B), this entry would likely score a 4. There is clear evidence of the principal's efforts to work collaboratively with families and staff to accomplish the renovation of the school. The description of the process is clear, although it lacks detail. It does indicate that many stakeholders were involved in the planning process. Effective use of media relations is evident in the description. However, evidence of the principal's professional growth throughout the process is weak. The analysis and reflection are superficial and lack the depth needed to raise this to a level 5.

Suggestions for Standard 4 Sample Artifacts
- A collection of newsletters demonstrating the candidate's expertise in communication with the community
- A video- or audiotape of the candidate speaking with a parent and community group
- A video- or audiotape of the candidate meeting with a small parent committee to address a specific community-based concern
- A meeting agenda and minutes of the candidate working with the school staff to implement an effective community interaction plan
- A video of the superintendent working with a community group to improve communication and prevent conflict

Part 4: Case Study, Standard 4

Read the scenario that follows and answer the questions at the end. Sample answers to each question are provided on the enclosed CD-ROM to guide you.

Marla Anthony is the principal of an elementary school in a suburban district. Recently, one of her teachers came to Marla with a request. This teacher has participated for the past three years in an electronic field trip program. The project utilizes satellite technology and the school's computer lab to link several classes of fifth grade students to a well-known historical site in another state. Marla's school was able to participate because the director of the district's high school radio and television program connected the school to the site. However, because of cutbacks in the budget, his position was eliminated. The district no longer employs anyone with the knowledge or ability to facilitate this project. Additionally, with the elimination of this position, the budget no longer provides for the subscription fee for this distance learning project. Recognizing the value of this learning experience for the students in her building, Marla has decided to seek the help of the community to try to maintain this project for her building. Marla has arranged a meeting with herself, the teacher who uses the distance learning project, and the president of the local cable television station. She hopes the cable company will agree to broadcast the live, interactive component of the project on a local cable station. Marla has already obtained a commitment from the school's parent support association to provide matching funds. The teacher is eagerly planning fundraisers to obtain the required half of the fee.

> *Question 1:* What artifacts related to this activity could Marla use to demonstrate that she has met Standard 4, Collaboration? Defend the choice of these artifacts by explaining how they illustrate the knowledges, dispositions, and performances that exemplify this standard.
>
> *Question 2:* Using the artifacts you selected in question 1, write a sample portfolio entry to describe, analyze, and reflect on Marla's attainment of Standard 4 as evidenced by this activity.
>
> *Question 3:* Apply the scoring rubric found in Appendix B to evaluate the first draft of your answer to question 2. Based on your application of the rubric, revise your sample entry. Describe why you made your revisions and explain how the changes strengthen the validity of your entry.

CHAPTER 5

Standard 5: Acting with Integrity and Fairness, and in an Ethical Manner

The well-being of students should be the fundamental value of all decision-making and actions.

—AASPA, 1988, p. 1

A school administrator is an educational leader who promotes the success of all students and staff by acting with integrity and fairness and in an ethical manner.

OBJECTIVES

The learner will

- Understand the complexities of ethics and school leadership
- Understand the difference between intrinsic and extrinsic ethics
- Reflect on several authentic vignettes of leaders struggling with ethical issues
- Practice the development of a portfolio entry
- Analyze a case study for further insight into attaining Standard 5

Part 1: Examining Standard 5

The Ethical Administrator

The Stereotype

Those who have been in the administrative ranks for any period of time know that many administrators operate from an ethical paradigm. Yet stereotypes of the "unethical" administrator abound. The question becomes, Where do these stereotypes originate? One might suspect that two major factors are at work: unethical past practice on the part of some administrators and the tendency of some administrators to focus on the pragmatic—that is, to do what it takes to get the job done regardless of the ethical considerations. And in this age of accountability, the internal and external influences that exist to focus on the pragmatic will only increase.

One of the key elements leading to the origins of unethical stereotypes seems to be a lack of direction regarding what administrative ethics are. In an international study of 552 building administrators conducted by Neil Dempster (2001), it was discovered that only

28% (155 administrators) had had any professional training in ethics, and most of it was at the university level. The remainder had had no training and no background. Yet the literature abounds with information on ethics and administration, and every major administration organization has codes of ethics for administrators: the AASA (American Association of School Administrators for Superintendents), the NSBA (National School Boards Association for School Board Members), and the NASSP or NAESP (National Association of Secondary, or Elementary, Principals for Principals). Obviously, there is no lack of information, so there must be some other explanation for this lack of direction. Certainly it would help if administrators had more professional training in the nature of and the practice of professional administrative ethics, but the critical factor is the one identified in Standard 5. A true sense of ethics is not something one will ever learn from a textbook; it is, rather, an internal attitude demonstrated in personal behaviors.

The Ethical Administrator as Defined in Standard 5

The 12 performances in Standard 5 are quite personal:

1. Demonstrates a personal and professional code of ethics
2. Demonstrates values, beliefs, and attitudes that inspire others
3. Accepts responsibility
4. Considers the impact of one's administrative practices
5. Uses the influence of the office to enhance, rather than for personal gain
6. Treats people fairly and equitably
7. Protects the rights and confidentiality of others
8. Demonstrates appreciation and sensitivity
9. Recognizes and respects
10. Welcomes and encourages
11. Fulfills legal and contractual obligations
12. Makes decisions based on ethical implications (For a complete list, see Appendix A.)

It is quickly noticeable that these statements are action statements. They do not require administrators to demonstrate knowledge; rather, they require administrators to demonstrate an innate sense of ethics in their behavior, values, beliefs, and attitudes. The best one may hope for from scholarship, therefore, is to develop a knowledge base and an understanding of what one is supposed to do. Certainly university and field training would assist administrators in developing this knowledge base, but it is not enough to meet the letter of Standard 5. For example, in Dempster's study (2001), participants demonstrated strong consistency in identifying personal attributes necessary for ethical decision making: "interpersonal skills; empathy; ability to fully recognize ethical features; reasoning and logic skills; knowledge of ethical principles; full knowledge of laws, rules, etc.; courage" (p. 14). Only two of these attributes are knowledge based; the rest are personal and would only be demonstrated by behavior.

Extrinsic Versus Intrinsic Ethical Behavior

If personal behavior is the key in Standard 5, how does one recognize whether one's behavior is based on ethical principles or on something else? For example, suppose a teacher lost her temper and physically pinned a student against a locker. The real issue is how to help both resolve the disagreement that led to the incident so that both have better tools to use in problem solving in the future. However, due to a fear of being sued, the administrator immediately disciplines the teacher for her physical excess. This allows the administrator to tell the irate parent (if such happens) that the ethical thing has been done in punishing the teacher. The essential issue—resolving the disagreement—has been postponed. In fact, the administrator is not occupied with thoughts of how to deal with problem resolution, but with whether the school will be sued. The administrator has attempted to demonstrate behavior that will convince people that an ethical standard was applied, when all that has really happened is that the administrator has protected the school from a potential lawsuit. The measure to apply here is whether the behavior is intrinsically or extrinsically motivated.

Extrinsic ethical behavior is behavior that is motivated by factors other than one's personal ethical beliefs. This behavior is not truly ethical behavior in the sense of Standard 5. Intrinsic ethical behavior is behavior that is motivated by one's innate sense of what is right and then acting according to that sense despite possible consequences. This behavior does meet the intent of Standard 5. It is not enough to point to behavior and claim it as ethical; it is necessary to examine the motivation behind the behavior to determine the degree to which ethics are at work. Others who observe our behavior certainly examine our motivations and are able to distinguish between behavior that is truly motivated by ethics and behavior that is motivated by extrinsic factors. In fact, this is a significant reason why these stereotypes exist. Therefore, leaders must continually examine their own beliefs and behaviors to determine whether they are motivated extrinsically or intrinsically.

It will not be an easy task to determine the difference between extrinsic and intrinsic ethical behavior, but guidelines do exist. For example, in Messer's (2001) review of ethical literature, he paraphrases Strike, Haller, and Soltis: ". . . responsible behavior and ethical behavior on the part of school administrators are synonymous concepts. They also maintain that educational leaders must develop the ability and capacity to consistently reflect about the ethics of their actions and decisions" (p. 16). He continues on his own: "The number and variety of actions and decisions made by school administrators in the course of one day is staggering. Although some of those might not appear to have ethical implications at all, I believe that school administrators are dealing with an increasing number of issues that require ethical reflection" (p. 16). Ethical reflection, then, will become the tool that administrators will use to determine the degree of intrinsic ethical motivation that they are displaying. The portfolio will be an ideal medium through which to practice such reflection.

Who Is an Administrator?

Up to this point, the word *administrator* has been used generically, but to whom should it refer? To whom should Standard 5 apply? The answer is that it should apply to all those who exercise administrative leadership: superintendents, principals, department heads, athletic directors, and, significantly, school board members. School board members sometimes have a tendency to regard themselves as somehow aloof from the administrative ranks. However, by state law, they are administrative leaders and are held accountable as such.

As an illustration of this fact, there was a recent lawsuit in New Jersey that clearly held school board members accountable to the state Code of Ethics in two different aspects of the same scenario (*Santiago* v. *Paterson Board of Education,* Passaic County, 2003).

One school board member filed a complaint with the school ethics commission against another school board member, accusing him of violating three different clauses of the Code of Ethics. The facts of the case were that an honors night was held for new students enrolling in the local community college. Some board members were in attendance, as was a mayoral candidate, but the superintendent of schools and the principal of the building where the ceremony was held, as well as other board members, were never notified or invited. After the ceremony at the reception, the mayoral candidate distributed campaign buttons.

One of the uninvited board members wrote a letter condemning the ceremony and accusing the invited board members of political maneuvering. One of the invited board members then filed the complaint against the accuser and it went before the School Ethics Commission. In a revealing decision, the Commission ruled that the event was indeed unethical, so it dismissed two of the three charges. However, it ruled against the defendant on the third. The problem was that, even though the accuser was correct in his accusations, he had sent copies of his accusatory letter to all board members, the superintendent, assistant superintendents, building principals, the state department of education, and the New Jersey School Boards Association. Building principals, however, are school employees under the board's supervision, so sending them copies of the letter was a violation of ethics. Personnel matters were not to be addressed publicly according to the Code. The result was that school board members had violated two different aspects of the Code of Ethics, even when one of them was correct. School board members are administrators and are subject to Standard 5 along with all other administrators. Therefore, the examples in this chapter and the performances, dispositions, and knowledges of Standard 5 should be considered applicable to anyone who holds an administrative position in a public school.

The remainder of this section is devoted to illustrations of ethical situations encountered by administrators and a discussion of how they should be addressed using intrinsic ethical behavior and Standard 5 performances. Obviously, these illustrations are not comprehensive; they represent a selection of cases that present a variety of situations in which administrators have demonstrated a range of ethical behavior.

Ethical Dilemmas of the Administrator

Teacher Security/Contract Issues

Dismissal of Nontenured Teachers.   During economically difficult times, job security for teachers has emerged as a major issue. This will only increase as new national and state standards raise the bar for expectations of new professionals entering the field. The school leader must assess and evaluate the abilities of these new professionals and, perhaps, weed some from the profession. This is not an easy task and it requires a school leader to exercise ethical considerations. As Messer (2001) learned when he conducted a study of the impact of dismissal of nontenured teachers on principals,

1. Teachers were not recommended for renewal primarily as a result of concerns about discipline, inappropriate behavior, and professionalism.
2. Principals were generally able to frame their decisions in context with their vision for the school.

3. Directors of school systems were generally supportive of principals making personnel decisions.

4. Personnel decisions frequently involved political considerations.

5. These decisions caused stress, anxiety, and emotional concerns for the principals.

6. The state model for teacher evaluation was generally considered as being inconsequential when making personnel decisions.

7. Few problems were encountered from "lame duck" teachers.

8. Principals frequently encouraged teachers to resign prior to taking formal action not to renew them.

9. Positive or benign letters of recommendation were frequently written for teachers who were not rehired.

10. A shortage of teachers has resulted in the hiring of nonrenewed teachers by other systems. (p. 2)

Focusing on entries 4, 5, 8, and 9 reveals a typical pattern of unethical behavior that reinforces the stereotype. Yet, there is often a benevolent rationale for why administrators do this. In the medical profession, one of the basic tenets is that a physician should first do no harm. School administrators believe in this tenet as well, but it is not so simple. Not rehiring a nontenured teacher, or firing a tenured one, results in harm. Yet continuing to employ an incompetent teacher also results in harm to students. Stress, anxiety, and emotional concerns are the result for the administrator who often attempts to mitigate the harm and assuage the conscience by attempting benign ways of easing the situation (as noted in entries 8 and 9). This is, however, a violation of ethics as noted in performances 1, 4, 6, 11, and 12 of Standard 5. Intrinsic ethical behavior requires the administrator to do the right thing even if the consequence is harm. To disguise the problem, or simply to transfer it to another school or district, is unethical behavior no matter how nobly conceived.

The tendency to avoid "harm" is even more pronounced when making decisions involving tenured teachers, because the amount of due process increases dramatically and the potential for stress, anxiety, and emotional concerns is eminently greater. According to Messer (2001), "The average cost to school systems that dismiss a tenured teacher has been reported to be as high as $500,000. . . . Not very many involuntary separations result in litigation, but most are contentious and sensitive" (p. 10). The administrator, therefore, sometimes attempts to use contract language to avoid confronting these issues directly.

Contract Issues.   As stated earlier, job security has become a major issue for teachers. Research has shown an increased concern on the part of teachers in contract language relating to reduction, transfer, and recall issues. Research in 1986 (Colon, 1989, 1990) discovered that seniority issues had increased by one third, transfer issues by one third, and staff reduction issues had doubled. This trend has continued as teachers have become more concerned with retaining jobs, with the result that school districts have had to pay much closer attention to contract clauses concerned with seniority, transfer, staff reduction, and recall. As these issues have increased in importance, administrators have become "creative" in attempting to manipulate contracts so that personal preferences in the retention of teachers can be "finessed." Not only is this unethical behavior, but courts and arbitrators have also soundly defeated such attempts. Colon (1989) discovered that administrators were losing grievance hearings by the rate of three to one.

An example of an attempt to manipulate the contract for personal reasons was *Zoll v. Eastern Allamakee Community School District* (1978); (Alexander & Alexander, 2001, p. 698). Mrs. Zoll (a teacher and former administrator) wrote several letters to the local newspaper criticizing administrative officials such as the superintendent and board members for making decisions that, in her opinion, emphasized athletics too much. She was called into the superintendent's office to discuss the letters and was chastised for her behavior. Shortly thereafter, the district had to reduce the faculty, so the administration created a 100-point system. Using this point system instead of seniority, Zoll's position was reduced. She protested the use of this point system, claiming that she had been denied rightful points and had, thus, lost her position. The board refused to relent, so she took the matter to court, where she won on the grounds that the "objective" point scale had been manipulated and she was unfairly fired, and, subsequently, was passed over on three separate occasions for recall.

Administrators need to understand, therefore, that there are no substitutions for behaving in an ethical manner. Performance 6 requires administrators to treat people fairly and equitably, performance 5 forbids the use of office for personal gain, and performance 11 requires the administrator to fulfill legal obligations. Leaders cannot allow their personal bias to interfere with ethical decision making. The intrinsically ethical decision here is not to manipulate the contract to eliminate someone with whom one does not agree.

Issues Relating to Constitutional Freedoms

Religious Issues—Teachers.   Religious issues are a particularly sensitive area because strong belief systems are involved on the part of everyone concerned. Performances 5 and 6 of Standard 5 emphasize that administrators must respect the beliefs of all school or district populations—teachers, students, parents, bus drivers, cooks, custodians, everyone. Administrators must not allow their own beliefs to influence behavior to the detriment of others. This is a difficult requirement to ask of any individual, but the administrator is a role model and must meet this requirement.

As an example of what happens when one loses sight of such a requirement, consider the "magic rock" case (1998) of *Cowan v. Strafford R-VI School District* (Alexander & Alexander, 2001, p. 823). Cowan, a second grade teacher, sent home on the last day of school a rock and a letter. Each time the students rubbed the rocks, they were supposed to think good things about themselves and were supposed to confirm the ability to accomplish whatever they desired. The principal criticized Cowan's use of the rocks and letters, and during the next school year, began issuing job targets to Cowan, thus indicating that her teaching was not altogether satisfactory. The principal addressed the entire faculty, expressing concerns about magic and "New Ageism." Ultimately, the principal indicated that Cowan had failed the job targets and recommended that the board not renew her contract, which subsequently the board did. Cowan took her case to court, where it was learned that the principal was influenced by local religious leaders who opposed the use of "magic" and pressured the principal to avoid "New Ageism" practices. The principal responded to these leaders and became a major factor in the board's decision to fire Cowan, accusing her of promoting a particular brand of New Age religion. The decision of the court was that Cowan had lost her job because of religious discrimination and they voted against the school district. Administrators must not allow themselves to be influenced by one community group to the detriment of an innocent party.

The same must be said of issues involving evolution vs. creationism; again, a very sensitive issue because of the strong beliefs on either side. Up to this point, the US Supreme Court has ruled that creationism is not a science and that evolution may not be banned from the curriculum. Many citizens are unhappy about these decisions and have attempted to influence school administrators to manipulate the law. However, whatever the beliefs of the individual administrator, the law may not be subverted, regardless of the intensity of community pressure. Intrinsic ethical behavior would require of the administrator that the law be followed, that the beliefs of all be considered within a legal framework, and that no matter how much easier it would be, one may not give into pressure.

In 1980, the Supreme Court ruled in *Stone v. Graham* (Alexander & Alexander, 2001, p. 195) that the Ten Commandments, being a religious text of the Jewish and Christian faiths, could not be posted on schoolhouse walls. Subsequently, there have been attempts to circumvent this ruling by such tactics as declaring the Ten Commandments a secular document and thus acceptable to post on the schoolhouse wall. Administrators must use their intrinsic ethical beliefs to sort the fiction from the truth and support the truth. The easy, and extrinsic, behavior is to "go along to get along" and follow the desires of the community.

Religious Issues—Students.   The same tenets of the previous discussion apply to students, with an important caveat. Because of compelling state interest, students must attend school, making them a captive audience. In addition, students are considered minors and are thus subject to influence by adults. Therefore, the principle of representing all becomes even more significant with regard to students. The administrator must represent all students and must remember that all students are minors who look to the administrator for protection and guidance. The issue of role modeling takes on added meaning as a result. The administrator must represent and protect all students, regardless of the administrator's own personal religious beliefs.

One of the issues that sorely tests this representation is that of school prayer. No one seems to have only a mild opinion on this issue. It can be extremely divisive for any school or district and requires of the administrator a strong ethical stance. The Supreme Court case *Lee v. Weisman* (1992; Alexander & Alexander, 2001, p. 202), for example, has become a very divisive force. In this case the Supreme Court ruled that prayer during graduation ceremonies is unconstitutional. This decision, not surprisingly, has run counter to the beliefs and wishes of many students and parents. There have been a number of attempts to circumvent this ruling with the collusion of school administrators. Administrators must remember that public schools represent a variety of religious beliefs and the administrator must support and protect all of them, not just the majority, which often means Christianity. Ethics require that one not use one's position to promote a personal brand of religion and, in fact, must protect all students from such behavior. Ethical behavior is not something that is demonstrated when it is convenient, but is something that is done because it is right.

Administrators without a firm understanding of personal ethics may also become drawn in to the controversy surrounding individual student prayer. There is a great deal of pressure on administrators to allow students to pray whenever students wish. It is easy to give in to this pressure, particularly since it is supported by parents. This is where a knowledge base is of great assistance to the ethical thinking of an administrator. Knowledge of the law would inform the administrator that it is legal for students to pray at any time as long as there is no disruption of the educational process and as long as no school employee attempts to influence such prayer. It is legal for the school to allow for a moment of meditation as long as there is no disruption and no school employee attempts to influence such mediation (*Wallace v. Jaffree,* 1985; Alexander & Alexander, 2001, p. 199).

Freedom of Speech Issues—Teachers.   Marvin Pickering, a teacher, sent a letter to a local newspaper criticizing the handling of finances by the board and the superintendent (*Pickering v. Board of Education,* 1968; Alexander & Alexander, 2001, p. 711). The letter was in connection with a proposed bond issue and was perceived as damaging to the cause of the school district. The board reacted by firing Pickering, asserting that his attack had been incorrect and insulting. Pickering, wishing to get his job back, took the issue to court and, at the Supreme Court level, won his case on the basis that simply because he was an employee of the school district, he was not to be denied his right to free speech. The court ruled that he has a right to speak on issues of public importance without fear of retaliation by the school district. Administrators are often criticized by employees, but must be ethical enough to realize the difference between legitimate exercise of legal rights and one's desire to retaliate when attacked.

Another censorship issue involves a classroom activity conducted by a teacher in which a profane term was used. Keefe, a teacher of senior English, assigned his class a magazine article in which a vulgar term for an incestuous son was used (*Keefe v. Geanakos,* 1969; Alexander & Alexander, 2001, p. 309). He informed his students ahead of time about the article and gave them an opportunity to do an alternate assignment. After the activity, he was called before the board, asked to explain his actions, requested to promise not to do it again, and, on his refusal to do so, was suspended pending dismissal. The Supreme Court ruled that the board was exercising unnecessary censorship. The teacher had a pedagogical reason for using the article, had notified students ahead of time, had allowed for alternate assignments, and therefore could not be censored simply because some board members did not like the term. Again, administrators must realize that the higher ethical good must sometimes supersede one's own personal preferences, because the administrator must represent everyone.

Freedom of Speech Issues—Students.   In this world in which we exercise individual rights, it becomes increasingly difficult to maintain a personal moral barometer, especially in the face of media pressure. It is that media pressure, however, that is, according to Grossman (1995), influencing our students to violent and dangerous behavior:

> The observation that violence in the media is causing violence in our streets is nothing new. The American Psychiatric Association and the American Medical Association have both made unequivocal statements about the link between media violence and violence in our so-

ciety. The APA, in its 1992 report BIG WORLD, SMALL SCREEN, concluded that the "scientific debate is over." (p. xvi)

Indeed, according to Kidder (2003), the extent of that pressure is clear in a Gallup Youth Survey finding that 67% of today's students aged 13 to 17 report a "great deal" or "a fair amount" of cheating goes on in their schools and 48% say they themselves have cheated on a test or exam.

It is little wonder, then, that students believe in complete freedom to write and speak as they see fit. The administrator must combine a strong knowledge base with an equally strong intrinsic ethical structure to determine how to support the law consistently while supporting the student's right to freedom of speech.

Supreme Court cases such as *Tinker v. Des Moines* (1969; Alexander & Alexander, 2001, p. 386), *Bethel School District v. Fraser* (1986; Alexander & Alexander, 2001, p. 389), and *Hazelwood v. Kuhlmeier* (1988; Alexander & Alexander, 2001, p. 401) have defined both student and school rights. Students have the right to express their constitutional freedom of speech, but the school has the right to maintain its educational mission. The trick for the administrator is to know the difference and not to let personal beliefs on censorship override ethical concerns. Sometimes this means allowing speech that one finds personally unappetizing. However, intrinsic ethical behavior means allowing that which is legal to exist without interference and that which is illegal to be censored. A knowledge base will help the administrator determine the difference. It is evident that a knowledge base is critical to the development of intrinsic ethical philosophy. One cannot make ethical decisions in a vacuum.

Another sensitive area for student issues is search and seizure. *New Jersey v. TLO* (1985; Alexander & Alexander, 2001, p. 415) defined the nature of search in public schools. An assistant principal searched a student's purse and discovered illegal substances that eventually led to charges. The student attempted to suppress the evidence, but the Supreme Court supported the administrator and defined the nature of search and seizure. The intrinsically motivated administrator will follow the law carefully, because the student does have due process rights that must be respected, and because all people are to be treated fairly and with dignity (performance 6). The law may not be twisted to allow the administrator to "catch" someone even when it might result in the removal of a serious problem for the administrator. It is especially important to treat individuals with respect during the most difficult of situations, because that is when most notice is taken. This is when the administrator's approach may garner the most respect.

Personal Morals Issues

Issues Involving New Standards.   Up to this point, most of the discussion has revolved around using ethics to make judgments about the behavior of others. However, it is of even more importance to use ethics to make judgments about oneself. For example, as new federal and state standards become more stringent and consequences more career threatening, administrators have been tempted to use their positions to cheat. In recent years in the Chicago area, there has been increased publicity on administrators who have been disciplined for using their positions to supply answer sheets to teachers, or for "creatively" scheduling those students whom they do not wish to take the standardized tests, or for pressuring their teaching faculty to teach to the test and have students memorize answers. Sometimes, this behavior is done for "benign" reasons; that is, administrators know that test scores are increasingly being tied to teacher job security and they are attempting to "assist" those teachers with that security. However, Standard 5 requires that administrators use "the influence of the office to enhance the educational program rather than for personal gain," even if that personal gain is for the benefit of others. Again, the test for intrinsic ethics is not expediency, but doing the right thing. Based on federal and state legislation, administrators are going to be increasingly pressed to make these ethical decisions. Sometimes it will be unavoidable to do harm in order to do the intrinsically ethical thing.

Sexual Harassment.   This is an issue in which courts are seeing increased activity. Becoming sexually involved with either employees or students is becoming one of the quickest ways out of the profession. Courts are holding administrators to a high standard of personal conduct. Being a role model for employees and students has assumed a high priority in this area. Because there are so many forms of sexual harassment today (i.e., teacher–teacher, teacher–student, student–student), the administrator must possess a powerful sense of self ethics to be able to adjudicate sexual harassment appropriately on the part of others. The old "boys will be boys" attitudes that courts first encountered on the part of administrators is no longer acceptable because of what it says about the personal ethics of the holder of such an attitude. As is the case for so many of the issues raised in this chapter, the personal ethics of the administrator will dictate how that administrator will interact with others. It is not enough for the administrator to apply the law on sexual harassment. It is necessary for the administrator to live the law. Applying the law because one is afraid of the consequences is extrinsic ethical behavior, but applying the law because one believes it is the right thing to do is intrinsic ethical behavior. One cannot treat someone with dignity and respect if one does not believe that sexual harassment is truly wrong.

Diversity Issues

Special Education.   Students who enter university educational administration training programs often have a myriad of views related to special education. Often these views are immersed in their own educational experiences, providing a rich foundation for dialogue. Informed dialogue should eventually focus on Standard 5, performance 8 (see Appendix A), which requires the administrator to "demonstrate appreciation for and sensitivity to the diversity in the school community." The special education population is increasing and is present in virtually every school district, so administrators must develop an appropriate knowledge base before making intrinsic ethical decisions. Many administrators delegate special education supervision to subordinates. This must be carefully considered because a sound first step for administrators who wish to think ethically about special education is to become acquainted with special education law and special education students. Study such sources as Alexander & Alexander (2001, pp. 438–497) for a knowledge base about special education and the law, for example, but become acquainted with special education students in the local district to understand the true meaning. Standard 5 places great emphasis on the necessity for administrators to demonstrate their intrinsic ethical values by demonstrating their acceptance of all people in the educational community.

Minority Students. In 1954, the US Supreme Court handed down one of the most significant court decisions in our country's history in the case of *Brown v. Board of Education of Topeka* (Alexander & Alexander, 2001, p. 504), in which the court nullified the separate-but-equal standard that had stood since 1896. This case was critical because it eliminated official discrimination against all minorities, thus opening the way for persons with minority backgrounds to become full and equal citizens. Following the Brown decision, there was much opposition to its implementation, but the court held firm and racial discrimination remains illegal to this day (Alexander and Alexander, 2001, pp. 498–547). However, it is one thing for the law to be on the books; it is quite another for the law to be implemented in schools on a daily basis. For this to occur, it is necessary to have administrators who do not merely follow the letter of the law out of fear of consequences, but who actually believe in the dignity of all people, the standard required by Standard 5, performance 8 (see Appendix A). It is therefore of crucial importance that administrators intrinsically believe in the worth and value of all people. Failure to do so will result in extrinsic ethical thinking at best (and an administrator who will have difficulty on the job). Increasingly, standards will not permit individuals to occupy positions of administrative authority without a demonstrated commitment to the value of recognizing the unique contributions of minorities in the schools and in the community.

It is important to note that the basic principles discussed in the previous paragraph are assuming important status once again in our society. Recent developments in desegregation and school funding issues at both federal and state levels are raising new concerns about the possible isolation of minorities and special education students. At the federal level, congressional acts and US Supreme Court decisions may have a profound impact on such isolation. The same may be said for similar activities at the state level. Administrators will, of necessity, have to be vigilant in preserving the hard-won lessons of the past in honoring the diversity that special education and minority students bring to the public school community.

Conclusion

The essential importance of Standard 5, of intrinsic ethical behavior, is that it transcends all the other standards. Without intrinsic ethical behavior, the other standards could not exist. Standard 1, for example, focuses on the "development, articulation, implementation, and stewardship of a vision of learning." In reading the performances that follow the definition, it is clear that ethical thinking permeates all of them. Goals cannot be set, a mission or vision cannot be developed, and all stakeholders cannot be involved without a clear ethical outlook.

Standard 2 promotes "advocating, nurturing, and sustaining a school culture and instructional program." Individuals "are treated with fairness, dignity, and respect." It is no accident that the same wording is found in performances in both standards. Student diversity is likewise celebrated in this standard as well as in Standard 5; again, no accident. The school culture, climate, and instructional program will not meet the demands of new accreditation standards without careful ethical decisions made by key administrators.

Standard 3 requires an administrator who succeeds by "ensuring management of the organization, operations, and resources for a safe, efficient, and effective learning environment." The performances stress implementation of the vision, the inclusion of stakeholders, and the practical processes for operating a school system. None of these, however, are possible without first considering the ethical implications of administrative behavior.

Standard 4 promotes "collaborating with families and community members, responding to diverse community interests and needs, and mobilizing community resources." Again, note the presence of respect to individuals and groups, to diversity, to partnerships, to stakeholders, to the community, to multicultural awareness, to gender sensitivity, and to racial/ethnic appreciation. All these issues are ethical issues; all of them have roots in Standard 5. No administrator will be able to accomplish these directives without an innate sense of intrinsic ethical behavior.

Standard 6 might as well be an extension of Standard 5. The administrator is admonished to succeed by "understanding, responding to, and influencing the larger political, social, economic, legal, and cultural context." All the performances are extensions of issues raised in Standard 5, and we again observe diversity, communication, and respect.

Standard 7 for district administrators focuses on "providing leadership in curriculum development, learning assessment, instructional supervision, and program evaluation conducive to student learning, staff professional growth, and district accountability." The performances heavily stress vision, diversity and stakeholders—all outgrowths of ethical thinking and behavior.

Standard 8, also for district administrators, has perhaps the most difficult task of all. This administrator is assigned the task of "recommending and implementing policy that guides district operations." Policies are the official ethical decisions made at the highest levels. They permeate all levels of the school community. It does no good for a building administrator to have a powerful intrinsic ethical philosophy if the policy makers at the top do not allow such a philosophy to have an impact on the actual business of the district. Lower level administrators are allowed to function because of the permission and support of higher level administrators, so intrinsic ethical behavior must begin at the policy-making level or the standards will have no impact.

So, how is an intrinsic ethical philosophy built? First, build an administrative knowledge base. The examples in this chapter serve to illustrate the thorough knowledge that an administrator must possess before even beginning to make ethical decisions. Ethical decision making cannot exist in a vacuum. Ideals, values, and beliefs based on misinformation or no information are what society knows as "prejudices." It is incumbent upon administration preparation programs to understand the standards thoroughly and base administrative preparation curricula on these standards and their performances, dispositions, and knowledges.

Second, build a knowledge base on ethical thinking and decision making. Dempster's 2001 study found that the 552 administrators queried preferred learning about ethical thinking in the following hierarchy:

- 53%, face-to-face delivery
- 51%, professional networking
- 42%, mentoring
- 20%, multimedia packages
- 11%, web-based delivery
- 7%, online learning (p. 15)

It is interesting to note that administrators much preferred some form of face-to-face interaction to technology-based interaction. Perhaps the rationale is that, as has been pointed out frequently in this chapter, one learns much about ethical decision making by observing people making such decisions in action. It is also worthy of note that many university programs, in an attempt to lure tuition-paying customers, have begun to implement complete web-based courses with no personal interaction, just the opposite of what seems to be the desired format.

Third, administrators must develop personal commitments to intrinsic ethical behavior. There is no instructional strategy for this step; it must be taken independently. Leaders must decide for themselves if they are motivated by extrinsic or intrinsic ethical considerations. But the truth is that administrators who find that they make decisions based on what's right rather than what's convenient will have the greatest chance to succeed given today's educational mandates. Another honest truth is that public education needs leaders who have an innate intrinsic ethical belief system. The choices that need to be made are going to be increasingly difficult and need to be made by those who have a solid intrinsic ethical philosophy that tells them who they are and how they should act. These people will make all the difference between those schools that fail and those that succeed.

Part 2: Key Performances, Knowledges, and Dispositions for Standard 5

Key Performances

All the performances for Standard 5 are important, but the following relate closely to the previous discussion of this chapter:

1. Demonstrate personal and professional codes of ethics
2. Demonstrate values, beliefs, and attitudes that inspire others to higher levels of performance
3. Consider the impact of their administrative practices on others
4. Use influence to enhance the educational program, rather than for personal gain
5. Demonstrate appreciation for and sensitivity to the diversity in the school community
6. Make decisions based on ethical implications

Personal/Professional Code of Ethics, Values, Beliefs, and Attitudes That Inspire Others

Combining the first two performances clearly demonstrates the nature of intrinsic ethical behavior. Ethical behavior begins with a personal, intrinsic philosophy of integrity and ethics. As the old adage says: "People may doubt what you say, but they will always believe what you do." Administrators must, first and foremost, demonstrate a personal code of ethics, a personal set of values is obvious to all segments of the public encountered. Leaders must not expect more from others than they themselves are willing to do. Administrators are the role models for everyone else in the school community and must act accordingly.

The Impact of One's Administrative Practices on Others

Another way to demonstrate intrinsic ethical behavior is always to consider the impact of decisions made on others. Recently, a local school administrator sent out a memo making a major change in the student dress code. Neither the faculty (who would have to enforce the change) nor the students (who would have to obey the change) were even aware that a change was being considered. The result was bad feelings all around, which eventually led to unfavorable media coverage and community controversy. The intrinsically ethical action would have been to involve those affected by the change (teachers and students) in planning the change.

Using Influence to Enhance the Educational Program

In this age of accountability, it would be easy to enhance one's personal reputation when test scores increase by taking credit or, conversely, to assess blame for decreases in scores. The temptation is also there to take ethical shortcuts to enhance the test scores to maintain one's personal reputation. The intrinsically ethical thing to do is to focus on the success of the educational program for its own sake, without consideration of its impact on personal career enhancement.

Appreciation for and Sensitivity to the Diversity in the School Community

This is a very emotionally charged ethical situation. Many people have very strong opinions and beliefs on such subjects as religion and politics. However, administrators cannot ethically allow personal beliefs to influence administrative decisions. No matter what the administrator believes personally about such issues as the Ten Commandments or prayer at graduation, the administrator represents all students and parents in the school population and must make no decisions that unfairly penalize those with differing viewpoints from the majority or from the administrator's own beliefs. This will require that the administrator must sometimes suspend personal beliefs in favor of being ethical toward those with whom the administrator might disagree.

Making Decisions Based on Ethical Implications

This performance represents the heart of the whole previous discussion about ethics. Intrinsic ethical decision making requires that decisions be made from an ethical standpoint, not a merely pragmatic one. If leaders are going to encourage or require change in instructional techniques in classrooms within their buildings, for example, they must do this for educational reasons, not because of pressure from the school board or from fear of being placed on the underachieving list. These are often very difficult decisions, but this is what ethics is all about—making difficult decisions for the right reasons.

Representative Comments Demonstrating Emerging Performances for Standard 5

- "What is in the best interest of everyone involved?"
- "I made a mistake. Here is what I am going to do to make it right."
- "How can I help?"
- "You are an outstanding administrative assistant. What can I do to make your job easier?"
- "I will attend the IEP meeting at 3:00. Is there anything I need to know about the student, his IEP, or his parents before the meeting?"

Representative Actions Demonstrating Emerging Performances for Standard 5

- The principal decides to retain Mr. Simmons as custodian even though there is a group of parents who have complained that he cannot speak English very well and should not be employed by the school.
- The principal has a personal code of ethics printed, framed, and displayed on the wall behind her desk.
- A courier arrives to serve Mrs. Mendez divorce papers. You ask him to wait until school is dismissed and the students have left the building before allowing him to serve the papers.

Key Knowledges and Dispositions

Previously this chapter demonstrated how an effective administrator would use the performances associated with Standard 5 to develop an ethical pedagogy. In addition to performances, Standard 5 contains knowledges and dispositions. This section will assist the administrator in understanding behaviors that demonstrate attainment of the knowledges and dispositions. The following lists detail those key knowledges and dispositions from Standard 5:

Knowledges
The administrator has a knowledge and understanding of

1. The purpose of education and the role of leadership in a changing society
2. The values, ethics, and challenges of the diverse school community
3. Professional codes of ethics

Dispositions
The administrator believes in, values, and is committed to

1. The ideal of the common good
2. The principles in the Bill of Rights
3. Bringing ethical principles to the decision-making process
4. Subordinating one's own interest to the good of the school community
5. Accepting the consequences for upholding one's principles and actions

6. Using the influence of one's office constructively and productively in the service of all students and their families
7. Development of a caring community

These knowledges and dispositions correspond closely with the performances discussed earlier. It is clear that Standard 5 expects school administrators to possess certain common intrinsically ethical performances, knowledges, and dispositions:

- A personal sense of ethics, values, beliefs
- An understanding of what administrative ethics are all about
- A personal set of behaviors that reflect an understanding of administrative ethics and a personal sense of ethics
- A demonstration to the entire community that the administrator believes in and protects the rights of all who have a stake in the educational community
- A demonstration in the belief that only through integrity and intrinsically ethical behavior will true school success be achieved

Representative Comments Demonstrating Emerging Knowledges/Dispositions for Standard 5

- "Good morning, faculty. As you know, the Board has approved an examination of how writing is infused in the curriculum K–12. You are the stakeholders most closely involved with the curriculum, so it is imperative to involve you in determining how we may indicate such infusion."
- "I understand that you wish the Ten Commandments to be posted on the walls of every classroom. However, not all our students recognize the Christian faith, so I must respect their beliefs by making certain we do not advance or endorse a singular form of religion."
- "I know that is what you wish me to do. However, I must first and foremost be true to my belief system, and what you ask is against my personal code of ethics."

Representative Actions Demonstrating Emerging Knowledges/Dispositions for Standard 5

- The principal makes certain that bullying and harassment of any kind are not only a violation of school rules but also a violation of the learning environment of the school and will not be tolerated.
- The principal refuses teacher requests to obtain copies of standardized tests and teach students the answers.
- The superintendent approves a building request allowing a student group to meet on the same conditions as other student groups even though personally opposed to the message of the group. The superintendent does this not because of the law, but because it is the fair thing to do.
- The superintendent refuses to discuss personnel issues (i.e., reasons for hiring or not hiring a specific teacher) with parents.

Specific steps for building the portfolio are discussed in the next section. In addition, refer to the accompanying CD-ROM for further activities related to Standard 5.

Part 3: Portfolio Exercise for Standard 5

The following exercise will help students seeking administrative licensure to build their professional portfolio. Procedures are described here that will lead to a completed entry for a professional portfolio (Standard 5). A five-level scoring rubric to measure the level of standard attainment is contained in Appendix B. The rubric provides the rater with scoring criteria to evaluate the portfolio exercise.

1. Access your file box and find the divider for Standard 5.
2. The following are examples of authentic situations in actual classrooms. Please read these and answer the questions provided.
   a. Scenario 1. You, the principal, have just spent an hour with a very abusive parent who has called you every name possible because of the suspension of his child. Eventually, you had enough and enforced the removal of the parent from the building.
      i. What is the ethical thing to do when faced with such a parent?
   b. Scenario 2. A regular education teacher in your building commented negatively about a special education student to another parent. These comments got back to the parent of the student. A lawyer visited the teacher/school/district and a lawsuit was filed.
      i. What are the ethical issues here?
      ii. What should the district administration do about this issue and the lawsuit?
   c. Scenario 3. The principal does not follow safeguard procedures for special education students and parents; holds conferences without notifying appropriate attendees; and tends to make decisions about special education students without notifying the appropriate faculty members and parents. The principal also buries requests for special education testing because of a concern about the cost of providing services.
      i. What are the ethical issues and what should be done about these behaviors?
   d. Scenario 4. The principal boosts test scores by arranging "detention" of those he does not wish to have in the testing session, and manipulates the testing dates of special education students for the same reason. The principal has also been known to promote a student to move the student out of the building.
      i. What are the ethical issues and what should be done about these behaviors?
3. Using these scenarios as a guide, consider an ethical dilemma that actually happened to you as part of your professional responsibilities. Write a reflection about what happened. Include in the description all the details (place, time, participants, but not specific names), what happened and why, and what you would do differently if you had the opportunity. Reflect on your personal participation and write about how this participation demonstrates your progress toward attainment of Standard 5, and how this participation demonstrates the involvement of leadership skills.

4. Provide written authenticity for the activity. Such authenticity would probably involve documents related to the scenario (remove all personal information).
5. Place the documentation with your record of the activity in one folder. Place the reflections and authenticity evidence in the two remaining folders.
6. Carefully review all the items and correct any errors.

A sample cover sheet and reflection narrative follow.

BOX **5.1**

Sample Portfolio Entry

Standard 5: Acting with Integrity and Fairness, and in an Ethical Manner

Artifact: Letters from the parents of a special needs student, notes from a case conference involving this student, letter from the Director of Special Services for Unified School District 19

February 17, 20XX

Eastside Middle School

Trima, MN

Artifacts

Throughout the first semester of this school year I have dealt with the concerns of the parents of a special needs student in my building. This student has been identified as learning disabled and has an individualized educational plan (IEP) that specifies the support services that the school will provide. The parents are dissatisfied with the level of services provided to their child. They have had their child privately tested by an educational consultant who is employed by a for-profit tutoring company. Based on the results of this testing, they have repeatedly requested additional services for their child, as is documented in letters that accompany this entry. The notes from the case conference provide documentation regarding the meeting of school personnel with the parents to discuss this matter. The letter from the director of special services addresses the manner in which I interacted with the parents during that meeting.

Reflection Narrative

Most parents want the best for their children, and I have great respect for those parents who are willing to be advocates for the needs of their children. It is unfortunate when the wishes of the parents come into conflict with the ability of the school to provide for those needs.

The parents of a learning disabled sixth grade student in my school believe that the child requires the one-to-one assistance of a paraprofessional learning aide. They have requested that such an aide be assigned to their child on a full-time basis. Their request is based on some testing that they had done at a for-profit tutoring center in our community. In the report, one of the observations made was that "(the child) learns best in a one-to-one instructional environment."

The student's IEP provides for daily direct reading instruction in the resource room. Additionally, the student may access the resource room for support with assignments in other classes. Accommodations are also specified for testing situations. As the notes from the case conference show, the resource room teacher, along with the director of special services and myself, repeatedly explained to the parents that we do not have the funds in our budget to hire a full-time aide for their child. If we were to do this, other children would not receive the services specified in their IEPs. Unfortunately, the parents became verbally abusive toward both the teacher and myself. Among other things, they accused the teacher of favoritism and claimed she spent too much time with other students and not enough with their child.

When the teacher became defensive, and it was apparent that the situation had the potential to deteriorate quickly, I called for an intermission. I asked the teacher to walk to the faculty lunchroom and purchase some soft drinks for everyone. While she was gone, I invited the parents to walk with me—"to stretch our legs"—down the main hall of the building. As we did so, I asked them to tell me some of the stories about their child's struggles and successes in school.

After listening to their stories, I commented that it was evident that they work hard at being good parents, and I commended them for their strong advocacy on their child's behalf. They visibly relaxed at this point. Our stroll had taken us to the doorway in front of the resource room, and I positioned myself so that the parents had a clear view of the students and staff working in the room. I pointed out to the parents that these other children also have parents who love them and want the best for them, but with the current resources available to us, increased services for their child meant decreased services for another child.

When the case conference reconvened, I directed the discussion toward ways that their child could be more effective in accessing the services of the resource room for assistance with work from other classes. There were some options available that the child was not utilizing, and the parents were unaware that their child was failing to request assistance from the resource room staff. Finally, the discussion turned to ways in which the parents could become advocates for increased special education funding.

The attached letter from the director of special services expresses her appreciation for the manner in which I worked with the parents and teacher to defuse a tense situation.

I firmly believe that it is important to honor the viewpoints of everyone by allowing each person an opportunity to "tell their story." At the same time, I am equally firm in my belief that this must be done in a way that respects the dignity of each participant in a discussion. Although I personally disagree with both the conclusions and the recommendations in the report that the parents provided, and while I question the credentials of the person who administered the private tests, I certainly acknowledge that the parents are trying to do the best thing for their child. Rather than telling the parents that we don't consider the recommendations of "outsiders," I encouraged them to discuss the report with us openly. Although they are still dissatisfied with the level of services their child is receiving, I hope they understand that I cannot and will not increase services to their child at the expense of other children.

Scoring Analysis for the Entry

Using the portfolio exercise scoring rubric (Appendix B), this entry would score a 4 or 5. The principal provided a clear explanation of the artifacts and the situation that called for the application of ethical decision making. It can be difficult to document how a leader responds to ethical dilemmas, but the choice of artifacts here seems to support the dispositions of Standard 5. A stronger reflection would have mentioned specific key elements of the standard and explained how the artifacts showed attainment of each element.

Suggestions for Standard 5 Sample Artifacts

- A personal essay outlining the candidate's commitment to ethics in all aspects of school leadership
- A letter from a staff member or community member explaining how the candidate demonstrated ethical behavior in a particular incident

(continued)

BOX **5.1**   **Continued**

- A collection of artifacts demonstrating the candidate's willingness to volunteer in the community
- A copy of a recent audit from the state commending the district's adherence to business ethics in financial management
- A letter from a member of the school board extolling the candidate's ethical behavior over a period of time

---

Part 4: Case Study, Standard 5

Read the scenario that follows and answer the questions at the end. Sample answers to each question are provided on the enclosed CD-ROM to guide you.

Teresa Watson is the principal of a rural, K–12 school that is undergoing significant renovations. In addition to building a new cafeteria, auditorium, and kindergarten wing, all the current classrooms are scheduled to be repainted, and new carpeting is to be installed throughout the building. Teresa is one of two finalists for a promotion to the position of assistant superintendent in her district. She was recently approached by a member of the school board, who informed Teresa that he would like to support her in her bid for this promotion. He then mentioned that his son-in-law recently opened a new business installing carpeting and could really use a few "big jobs" to help him get the business off the ground. Although nothing was said overtly to imply that Teresa should award the bid for carpeting to the board member's son-in-law in exchange for his vote, Teresa had the clear impression that this was the deal being offered by the board member.

> *Question 1:* What is the ethical way for Teresa to respond to this situation?
>
> *Question 2:* Should Teresa make others, such as the superintendent and other members of the school board, aware of this conversation?
>
> *Question 3:* If the bid submitted by the board member's son-in-law is actually the best bid for the contract, should she award the bid to him? Why or why not? How should she handle this with the board member?

Standard 6: The Political, Social, Economic, Legal, and Cultural Context

School authorities are vested with broad powers for the establishment and conduct of the educational program. This prerogative, however, is by no means absolute and school officials must act within the scope of reasonable rules and regulations.

—Alexander & Alexander, 1998, p. 291

A school administrator is an educational leader who promotes the success of all students and staff by understanding, responding to, and influencing the larger political, social, economic, legal, and cultural context.

OBJECTIVES

The learner will

- Understand the complex aspects of the school's political, social, economic, legal, and cultural environment
- Understand the importance of policies such as diversity
- Understand how to demonstrate the knowledges and dispositions associated with Standard 6
- Practice completing a portfolio sample
- Analyze a case study and create new understandings about attaining Standard 6

Part 1: Examining Standard 6

The many contexts that influence education are found in varying degrees from school to school. Yet in any educational setting, a school leader's success is tantamount to a sound awareness and understanding of five crucial contexts (i.e., political, social, economic, legal, and cultural). To understand these multiple educational contexts fully, school administrators must apply a consistent taxonomy with which to view these competing, complementing, and transformational influences. This chapter organizes the five contexts for purposes of clarity, keeping in mind the guiding principles that school leadership is changing, aligned, collaborative, and must reflect the centrality of student learning. The chapter's organization will provide a mechanism to rationalize and understand school governance, democracy, educational law, change and conflict, global issues and forces, policy development and advocacy, and diversity.

Public School Governance

The very basis of school governance is rooted in the US government's federal, not national, system. A federalist system relies on a vertical diffusion of power from the federal to the state and local levels of government (Alexander & Alexander, 1998). Included in this federalist belief is the specific intent that education be founded on the constitutions of the 50 states and the federal government. Our nation's founding fathers feared a centralized system of education (i.e., a national education system) might jeopardize our democratic freedoms by advancing a single doctrine or perspective. To prevent this, the US Constitution does not specifically mention education, allowing state constitutions to establish distinct educational systems. As one might expect, education and attendant governance structures vary from state to state. Regardless of the vast differences, some things remain constant. The local school district, including all schools in its charge, is considered the basic governmental unit. Powers afforded the local school district, its elected or appointed officials, and school administrators are derived from state constitutions.

Local school boards, central office administrators, and building administrators form a district's leadership–governance structure and have historically been empowered to operate the schools in the district. In recent years, empowerment has assumed a different meaning, in which a conceptual shift occurred that is now more focused on outputs than inputs. Central to this shift is student success. The role of school governance is rapidly being redefined under this new focus, having strong implications for change. No longer can school governance structures operate in isolation. Connections with diverse groups of stakeholders at the local, state, and national levels are essential if output measures are to be meaningful. The key to meaningful measures is alignment. School governance structures must ensure that output measures (e.g., student success, program assessment and evaluation, dropout and attendance rates, adequate funding) are aligned among schools within the district, districts among the state, and with state and federal expectations.

For school governance structures to ensure meaningful, aligned output measures that are central to student success, the roles of stakeholders are clear. Elected or appointed school board officials assume a policy development role that furthers the educational interests of the district and its students. The superintendent and central office administrators provide the necessary leadership, in accordance with school board policy, to promote the educational interests of the district and to ensure student success. District leaders and school board members must also establish a climate and culture that supports these interests and procures resources that further this commitment. The building administrator, charged with the district's educational interests and necessary resources, then provides leadership for the particular school to ensure student success.

Building administrators deal primarily with school–community stakeholders at the local level to build capacities for student success. This includes faculty, staff, students, parents, and others in the community. Building leaders have a school leadership–governance responsibility to work with these stakeholders to develop a mission, vision, and goals that are aligned with the district, but are unique to school needs. With regard to leadership–

governance, some may argue that collaborative efforts are inefficient uses of time and result in groups of policy makers, not stakeholders. However, student success cannot be achieved until collaboration is central to the climate and culture of school governance.

Democracy

Governance structures, although based on federalism, are also founded on democratic principles. That is to say, all citizens of this nation are guaranteed certain freedoms, such as life, liberty, and property based on consent of the governed (i.e., by the people and for the people). School board officials and school leaders, as a part of governance structures, are bound by these same democratic principles. However, just because schools and districts embrace collaborative and engaging processes involving broad groups of stakeholders as a school governance cornerstone, democracy is not guaranteed. Simply stated, a democratic process does not ensure a democratic outcome. The democratic outcome relies on the individuals who compose the governance structure. This individual reliance on democratic outcomes has strong implications for moral leadership and effective leaders embracing democratic principles.

Students have a constitutional property right to an education. Moreover, the right to an education mirrors the same democratic freedoms afforded our nation's citizenry. Critics of our nation's diffused educational system often say it is impossible for *all* children to learn. These critics claim it is too expensive, erodes high standards, and discourages educators. Yet, the moral compass of school leaders would point to the fact that *all* children have the right to learn and the challenges presented in ensuring success for *all* students cannot detract from the democratic benefits afforded these students. A moral compass is the school leader's value-added leadership dimension (Sergiovanni, 1997) in which clear decisions are few and often competing with other demands.

A commitment to democratic principles is a challenging, but necessary, step for school leaders. In an era of competing resources, high-stakes accountability, and choice, how does the building leader practice democratic leadership? School leaders can

- Model leadership that is not self-serving
- Involve broad and diverse groups of stakeholders in decision making
- Establish ground rules for group involvement and adhere to them—remember, they are stakeholders, not policy makers
- Support a school climate and culture that is participative, collaborative, and dedicated to student learning
- Recognize and value the federalist nature of schooling (i.e., vertical diffusion of power). A school's outcomes must be aligned with the district, other schools, and state and federal expectations; democratic schools do not operate in isolation.
- Develop a collaborative and aligned vision, mission, and goals for their school
- Dedicate their leadership and resources to realizing the vision, mission, and goals

Leadership for schools can be nothing more than a powerful manipulation tool. An adherence and commitment to democratic principals ensures *all* stakeholders the life, liberty, and property interests an education was intended to provide.

The application of democratic principles in a pure sense could be very costly in terms of resources such as time and money. School leaders must be sensitive to resource allocation. Time and money should be recognized and valued by school leaders as scarce resources. How resources such as time and money are utilized has both political and economic implications. Swanson and King (1997) provide a material resource clarification that squarely addresses such resources. They note:

> Politics—the process by which values are allocated within society—differs from economics—the study of the allocation of scarce resources within society. Economics is concerned with the production, distribution, and consumption of commodities. Achieving efficiency in the use of resources is the highest objective of economics—where efficiency is defined as securing the highest level of societal satisfaction at the least cost of scarce resources. Obviously, one's value priorities strongly influence one's judgment as to what is an efficient allocation of material resources. Thus, there is a continual interaction between economics and politics. (p. 1)

The interaction to which Swanson and King (1997) refer is indicative of the competing demands frequently placed on school leaders. Resource decisions that support political values may impede economic efficiency. Likewise, economic gains may conflict with a school's political values. Additionally, the efficient allocation of time and money is strongly value laden. Effective leaders can balance the economic and political pressures that exist in schools, finding creative ways to allocate precious resources such as time and money. Whether considerations for resource allocation are economic, political, or some balance of the two, democratic principles that support student learning must underscore school leadership.

Educational Law

Educational law is a comprehensive and complex discipline. Effective school leaders garner a sound understanding of the legal system and its judicial influences on schooling. Although a short discourse on the legal context provided in this chapter cannot encompass the full body of law, the guiding principles may offer useful insights into effective school leadership.

The American educational system has been designed to educate its citizenry. Although this task may seem daunting, Essex (2002) notes that educational leaders must increasingly use discretion to make rational and legally defensible decisions within this system (2002, p. xix). Given the diversity of students served and the uniqueness of our decentralized systems from state to state, two assumptions must be understood. First, differences and conflict will occur among school stakeholders that are not resolvable through normal school governance channels. In these cases, judicial intervention is necessary. The outcomes of these judicial proceedings at every level (i.e., local, state, and federal) provide valuable knowledge that informs school leaders. The second assumption is intimately tied to the first. No single rule or "law of the land" exists among the differing educational systems in the country. With each state's constitution uniquely defining education, judicial rulings must be understood in the context with which the ruling occurred. This does not, however, negate a ruling's importance, because generalizing serves to inform school leadership. Care must be taken, though, to understand thoroughly the context of each ruling if a fair interpretation is to be made.

The legal context is a sound reminder that education and school leadership remain in constant states of change. A thorough historical perspective of school law is an essential school leadership tool, but legal currency is equally important. Because of the federalist and political nature of education in America, judicial outcomes are conflicting, competing, and ever changing. Effective leaders understand this legal challenge as they review historical perspectives and seek currency through recent judicial outcomes.

Often overlooked in the legal context is the importance of relationships. Effective school leaders foster meaningful, value-laden relationships with school–community stakeholders. As these relationships strengthen, the character of the school leader strengthens, serving as an effective tool to minimize judicial intervention when conflict and differences occur. A breakdown of meaningful, productive relationships is often the cause of judicial intervention. Wise school leaders will invest in healthy school–community relationships, using their understanding of the legal context as a guide to negate and minimize judicial intervention. School leaders must model this relationship investment to affect the school's climate and culture in similar ways.

As school leaders review and remain current in educational law, the temptation exists to reduce the legal context to right or wrong, legal or illegal. A closer examination of the judicial proceedings usually reveals a relationship breakdown early in the conflict or disagreement. Effective school leaders find proactive, preventative ways to minimize judicial intervention rather than respond to disputes as right or wrong, legal or illegal. As effective leaders model these proactive, preventative behaviors, stakeholders will be discouraged from reducing the complexities of schooling our nation's students.

Change and Conflict

Effective leaders understand there are numerous change forces, both internal and external, that influence schooling. They also understand some change is planned and other change is unplanned. Because planned change can be challenging and unplanned change cannot be predicted, school leaders must nurture cultures that are responsive to all changes. Cultures, by their very nature, are resistant to change and harbor tenacious characteristics that thwart change. Often missing in ineffective schools are agents of change. Conversely, effective schools most often have leaders who serve as change agents.

As with the other contexts described in this chapter, change does not occur in isolation. It is a competing context that influences the others. Change agents understand the competing nature of change and offer a systemic perspective rather than an isolated one to ensure meaningful and lasting change. Sergiovanni (2001) notes:

> A systems view provides a dynamic, integrative, and powerful view of change. Within this view, the unit of change is not limited to the individual teacher, the school, the workflow of teaching and schooling, or the broader political and administrative context. Instead, the four are viewed as interacting units of change, all requiring attention. When attended to properly, these units of change are the roads to successful school improvement. (p. 313)

Effective change agents are distinct from others largely because they understand the collaboration required to foster a systemic view of change. Genuine collaboration aims at the heart of a school culture, often challenging the school–community's collegial relationships. Lunenburg and Ornstein (2000) best provide the charge of the effective school leader serving as a change agent through a school culture paradigm:

> Every organization has its own culture, and the school is one of the most powerful factors for determining collaboration or lack of it among teachers and administrators. The school's culture in part determines what is important: how things are done, who does what, and what aspects of teaching, curriculum, and instruction are rewarded. In the final analysis, collaborative efforts must be valued, sanctioned, and supported by the administration. (p. 471)

Inexorably tied to change and collaboration is conflict. The interactions of school–community stakeholders are central to collaborative change efforts. These interactions embody a diverse set of values, opinions, beliefs, and assumptions. Conflict results when disagreements arise. Although too much conflict may be harmful, conflict as a constructive outcome of interactions is healthy and stimulates change. As with change, dealing with conflict must be embodied in the heart of a school's culture. Effective leaders understand this and foster cultures that encourage the sharing of differing values, opinions, beliefs, and assumptions in ways that stimulate meaningful change. Similarly, DeCenzo and Silhanek (2002) note that viewing conflict situations through the eyes of stakeholders minimizes conflict.

As school leaders build capacities within their schools to support a vision, mission, and goals for student learning, change will be necessary and conflict will arise. Nothing could more sharply illustrate the healthy nature of change and conflict than when dealing with the centrality of student learning. At the core of student learning changes, conflict will naturally arise as existing teaching and learning paradigms are challenged, power structures are questioned (e.g., a shift from teaching to learning, and inputs to outputs), existing knowledge and skills prove insufficient, the school's organizational structure is reviewed, and resources are realigned. Effective leaders focus on collaborative school cultures to meet the challenges of change and the resultant conflict that will improve student learning.

Global Issues and Forces

Education plays a key role in understanding and responding to globalization. Aligning economies, social influences such as mobility, and access and availability of information have illuminated the global context. As our nation's school communities diversify, so will their values, beliefs, and assumptions. Effective leaders are aware of the global dimensions impacting their schools and understand a contextual perspective that is more comprehensive than simply learning about "global issues."

Although global influences at the local level are uniquely different, school leaders must invest their time and resources in developing an understanding of how globalization is affecting their school–community cultures. A central theme that permeates these cultures is interdependence. Individual and collective decisions of school–community stakeholders impact global society. This is most apparent when considering the centrality of student learning and the scope of domestic and foreign contributions students will make during their lifetimes.

The competing nature of choices (e.g., to accomplish one goal may mean to impede another) implies that school–community stakeholders cannot function in isolation, nor are their decisions discrete. A focus on collaborative efforts fosters the development of organizational capacities that support a culture of interdependence. To achieve collaboration, stakeholders must agree on goals and how they will be achieved. This alone can be a daunting task, yet it fosters relationships that are supportive and systemic. Cornerstones of successful interdependence include supportive (i.e., value-laden) relationships and a systems perspective. Conflict, inherent to competing choices, is also part of the collaborative process. As collaborative school communities seek ways to minimize conflict, they also identify healthy ways for conflict to spur innovation and initiate change.

The very visions and missions of our nation's schools compel school leaders to develop broader school capacities that consider global issues and forces. Visions and missions provide our schools' educational dreams and how these dreams will be achieved. They often include phrases like "all children," "global society," and "globally competitive." If these stated phrases are genuinely guiding student learning, the global context must be considered. School visions and missions are also crafted around current and emerging trends such as accountability, choice, adequacy of funding, and shifts from inputs to outputs. These examples are only a few of the many undeniable forces facing our schools that are influenced by globalization. Hanvey (1982) offers five global perspectives that assist school leaders in understanding the cultural influences of globalization as well as a contextual dimension for building global capacities. These perspectives have implications for all school–community stakeholders.

1. *Perspective consciousness:* This is recognition that stakeholder views of the world are not shared by others, and an awareness that their views are directly or indirectly shaped by global forces.
2. *"State of the world" awareness:* Stakeholders must acquire current knowledge about world conditions and trends, and the existing political/economic/social forces.
3. *Cross-cultural awareness:* Effective participation in an interdependent world means participating in any culture from a global perspective. To do so means to become knowledgeable about existing cultures and their perspectives, relate to individuals from varying cultural backgrounds, and perceive others as individuals who create culture.
4. *Conceiving and thinking of the world as a global system:* Stakeholders must understand a "systems" approach to thinking and acknowledge the existence of global systems.
5. *Awareness of human choice and opportunities for action:* Participation in a global system means making competent and informed decisions, and identifying and engaging in alternatives. (p. 162)

School leaders who do not facilitate the capacity for growth for a global perspective deny school–community members opportunities for collaboration in a value-laden environment and minimize the access and awareness opportunities associated with interdependence. Lacking a global perspective, school visions and missions are narrowly defined and treat student learning as a discrete function.

Policy Development and Advocacy

School leaders have an obligation to ensure advocacy for the students they serve. Simply stated, advocacy is the protection and promotion of a school's most precious resource—its children. Effective school leaders create capacities within the school community that serve as the voice of their students at the local and state levels. This voice clearly communicates that an investment in a child's education provides essential resources for the complex needs facing our children. This cannot, however, be accomplished by the school leader alone. School leaders can develop advocacy capacities by focusing on collaborative opportunities that involve broad groups of diverse stakeholders focused on students and student learning. Only then can the complex advocacy needs of the student be understood. Advocacy must also include an understanding of the families of students as well. If advocates want to ensure students are succeeding at school, understanding a family's capacity to support education is essential too.

Nothing may be considered more competitive than the resources expended by governmental entities, including state legislatures and local school boards. These governmental units are comprised of elected and appointed officials at the local and state levels who serve in a policy development and resource allocation role. Their stated policies, ranging from legislative and administrative to local board policy, guide the operations of the units they represent. These officials also determine resource allocation based on the needs of the constituents they serve. Competing demands often create difficult resource decisions. Advocacy includes an understanding of these political and competing environments, articulating student needs and interests for officials, and influencing policy development and resource allocation for students and their families.

As capacities for advocacy grow within a school, an issue with which the school leader will undoubtedly grapple is which concerns, of the many, should be considered priorities. The National Association of Child Advocates (2003) offers a 10-step selection process to prioritize advocacy issues and strategies:

1. Defining and documenting the problem
   a. What is the problem and its severity?
   b. How many students are affected?
   c. Has the problem been observed and analyzed elsewhere?
2. Relationship of issue to the advocacy organization
   a. Has this issue been addressed by our school or by any other organization before?
   b. Is this an issue that our school wants to or should be addressing?
   c. Is it desirable or feasible for us to explore this issue given our current capacities?
   d. Do we want to lead, cosponsor, work in coalition, or simply endorse the actions of others?
3. Relationship of the issue to other organizations
   a. Who are the stakeholders on this issue?
   b. Have any other organizations identified this issue?

    c. If so, have their efforts been effective?

    d. Is there a unique or distinctive contribution we can make?

    e. Can we build new networks or coalitions for future efforts?

    f. Are we involved in too many initiatives?

4. Remedies sought and outcome expected

    a. What are the specific changes, stated in measurable outcomes for students, sought by our school?

    b. What will be necessary to achieve these changes?

5. Resources and timing

    a. What resources are available that can be focused on this issue?

    b. What additional resources would be needed, and if currently available, how can they be secured?

6. Strategy for change

    a. What strategies will be employed?

    b. What is the optimal strategy—the most direct, simple, and cost-effective?

7. Selecting the issue

    a. Have we seriously considered alternative policies or programs to determine whether we have selected the best one?

    b. Have other organizations addressed this issue, and what were their experiences and lessons learned?

8. The likelihood of support

    a. Will school–community stakeholders support this?

    b. Will other stakeholders support this?

    c. Can all stakeholders easily identify with the students in need of advocacy?

    d. Can we express the issues in a way that generates concern?

    e. Does the issue contain diversity (i.e., racial or ethnic) issues that may impact the outcome?

    f. How will this issue fit into the other contexts?

    g. What is the media's role?

9. Priorities

    a. Does the issue address the students in greatest need?

    b. Does the issue provide sufficient reason to reevaluate our priorities?

10. Outcomes

    a. How is the outcome likely to affect us?

    b. Can we leverage our participation to increase resources, membership, reputation, clout, and school–community outreach? (pp. 1–2)

The preceding questions have strong implications for school leadership. A collaborative culture must exist that encourages the honest responses to these questions. Honest responses also require a decision-making process to be in place. Decision making, especially with regard to questions of advocacy, must be clear and specific, based on reliable information, and well structured. Otherwise, decisions are less likely to be credible and may be wrought with emotion and judgment. The more emotion and judgment are relied on in decision making, the less policy and procedure is utilized.

Diversity

The context of diversity cannot be understated as a critical influence. Diversity has been conceptualized and defined in many ways, both theoretical and practical. Although diversity has mere curricular and instructional overtones for some educators, it serves as a source of pedagogy at the foundational and disciplinary core for others. Many school leaders will define diversity by ethnic and racial demographics, whereas others view poverty and mobility as highly diverse measures. Still others believe diversity to be defined as the broad values, beliefs, and assumptions that form the complexion of school–community stakeholders.

Regardless of these varying definitions and conceptualizations, DeCenzo and Silhanek (2002) note that diverse groups in a common setting rarely form a single group, but rather congregate with others sharing similar backgrounds and characteristics. School leaders should ask the following questions as a basis to identify and define diversity in their schools:

- Are access, opportunity and empowerment of school–community stakeholders actively practiced (Council of Chief State School Officers, 1996)?
- Does the existence of a value-laden culture permeate education?
- Does the school provide an education for *all* students?
- Are appropriate curriculum and strategies utilized?
- Is there an educational focus on equality and adequacy?

These competing and complementary questions may be thought of as diversity dimensions that contribute, in varying degrees, to a more robust conceptualization and definition of diversity. Figure 6.1 depicts this relationship. Unique school–community interpretations of diversity will not be fully realized until all dimensions are understood and accepted. These dimensions remain static only as long as their influencing factors are constant. Diverse influences, however, are constantly changing, requiring ongoing assessment.

The heart of educational diversity centers on whether the school community is committed and believes *all* children can learn. When the vision and mission includes "all children," and "all children" are central to learning, diversity is acknowledged and at least partially understood. The "all-children" dimension must be embedded in the very culture of the school community or it is simply words without action. Cultures, like diversity, are difficult to define. However, it is known that effective school leaders foster cultures that are value laden. When diverse values are acknowledged, encouraged, understood, and cultivated within the school community, healthy cultures form. Access, opportunity, and empowerment of school–community stakeholders strengthen capacities for diverse awareness and understanding. These actions, combined with the belief that *all* children can learn, and embedded in a value-laden culture, form an emerging picture of diversity.

Commonly referred to in judicial reviews of finance, equity and adequacy may also be thought of as fairness and sufficiency respectively. Effective school leaders understand the competing and complementary nature of these diversity dimensions and deliberately reflect on which paradigm (i.e., equity or adequacy) is most appropriate, if not both. These terms have implications for diversity that reach far beyond resource allocation. Equity and adequacy also deal with programs and core educational operations. However, without the

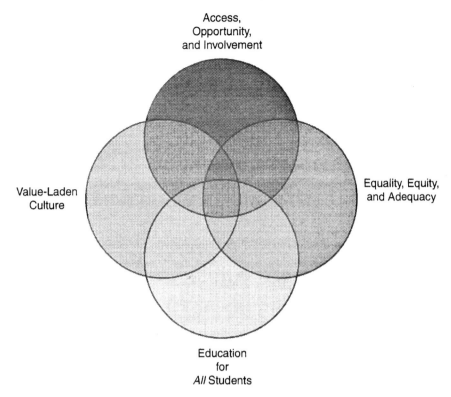

FIGURE 6.1   The Competing and Complimentary Dimensions of Diversity The overlapping dimensions form an ever-changing definition of diversity.

other dimensions of diversity, equity and adequacy are simply tools for the judiciary, leaving potential disparities among the other dimensions.

Part 2: Key Performances, Knowledges, and Dispositions for Standard 6

Key Performances

The beginning of this chapter provided the political, social, economic, legal, and cultural contexts of leadership. However, the performances are clearly action oriented, requiring administrators to "facilitate" specific processes. Cunningham and Gresso (1993) note that facilitation creates a collegial environment, fostering personal growth and improvement on a continuing basis. Cunningham and Cordeiro (2000) more specifically discuss the major roles of a facilitator:

- Build capacities and stature of group members
- Nurture diverse values and perspectives among group members

- Create ownership among group members
- Nurture creative thoughts of others
- Ask questions that help members rethink positions
- Ensure that team members identify resources, outside information, and ideas needed to address the problem
- Use effective, solid, time-tested group processes to maximize the efficacy of the group and its individual members
- Demonstrate effective listening, processing, and communication skills
- Encourage goal-directed behavior, and foster a patient and encouraging environment (pp. 374–375)

Facilitation and its robust implications are the clear and distinctive charge of administrators when considering the performances of Standard 6.

Performances
The administrator facilitates processes to encourage that

1. The political, social, economic, legal, and cultural environment in which schools operate is influenced on behalf of students, their families, and staff
2. Communication occurs within the school community concerning trends, issues, and potential changes in the environment in which schools operate
3. There is the opportunity for ongoing dialogue with representatives of diverse community groups
4. The school community works within the framework of policies, laws, and regulations enacted by local, state, and federal authorities
5. Public policy is shaped to provide quality education for students
6. Lines of communication are developed with decision makers outside the school community

Representative Comments Demonstrating Emerging Performances for Standard 6

- "If politics defines the process by which values are allocated within society, how do politics influence our teaching and learning? Similarly, how does education influence politics?"
- "Do our student rules compete with our vision and mission statements? Can we serve *all* children with staunch suspension/expulsion policies?"
- "Does a zero-tolerance policy reflect favorably on our vision for teaching and learning?"
- "Although the court ruling occurred in a different federal circuit court than ours, what does it mean for our school practices?"
- "I realize there are conflicting views, but this discussion is healthy and will no doubt produce an informed outcome."
- "What external forces are currently shaping our decisions regarding this policy? Should we be responsive to these forces and why?"

- "Please ensure your professional development request is directly linked to our school improvement plan."

Representative Actions Demonstrating Emerging Performances for Standard 6

- Administrators understand that blaming state and federal agencies for "mandates" communicates a message of powerlessness and lack of control regarding teaching and learning, which is an unhealthy climate characteristic.
- Administrators recognize that parent/community involvement is a cornerstone of meaningful school improvement.
- Administrators support both one-way (e.g., newsletters) and two-way (e.g., face-to-face, town hall forums) means of communication to strengthen school–community relations.
- Principals ensure that committees frequently have "at-large" representatives to invite the input of external stakeholders with diverse perspectives.
- Superintendents foster a climate and culture that is responsive to the diverse needs of the local school community.

Key Knowledges and Dispositions

Previously this chapter demonstrated how an effective administrator will use the performances associated with Standard 6 to develop the political, social, economic, legal, and cultural contexts of leadership. In addition to performances, Standard 6 contains knowledges and dispositions. This section will assist the administrator in understanding behaviors that demonstrate attainment of the knowledges and dispositions. The following lists detail the key knowledges and dispositions for Standard 6:

Knowledges
The administrator has a knowledge and understanding of

1. The law as related to education and schooling
2. The political, social, cultural, and economic systems and processes that impact schools
3. Models and strategies of change and conflict resolution as applied to the larger political, social, cultural, and economic contexts of schooling
4. Global issues and forces affecting teaching and learning
5. The dynamics of policy development and advocacy under our democratic political system
6. The importance of diversity and equity in a democratic society

Dispositions
The administrator believes in, values, and is committed to

1. Education as a key to opportunity, social mobility, and self-realization
2. Recognizing a variety of ideas, values, and cultures
3. The importance of a continuing dialogue with other decision makers affecting education
4. Actively participating in the policy-making context in the service of education

5. Using legal systems to protect student, staff, and parental rights

Key Knowledges

A systemic approach to schooling is encouraged through the principal's leadership to minimize a culture of isolation and encourage interdependence. It is modeled through highly visible means, such as allocating resources (e.g., time and money) and using a decision-making framework, especially when dealing with conflict.

The legal context of schooling is never reduced to right/wrong or legal/illegal, which is a low-trust perspective. Rather, the legal context serves as a guide for good-faith efforts to build strong relationships, reflecting a high-trust perspective.

These systemic considerations will manifest themselves in ways that form a clear agenda for the advocacy of teaching and learning, immersed in a culture of democracy. To consider these systemic challenges is to focus on the common good with a genuine and meaningful commitment to engaging diverse stakeholders.

Representative Comments Demonstrating Emerging Knowledges for Standard 6

- "Understanding and implementing a schoolwide risk management program will allow us an efficient means to address several recent legal changes."
- "Let's ensure enough time is taken to collect and document evidence that supports implementation of this school improvement initiative. Please understand that meaningful change doesn't happen quickly and sound evidence allows us to address change by understanding what is working and what is not."
- "A shift from inputs to outputs is very similar to a shift from teaching to learning. What implication does this have for our school?"
- "Do our vision, mission, and goal statements focus on inputs or outputs?"
- "Our vision statement uses the term *global* twice. What does 'global' mean to our school community? In what ways are teaching and learning at our school globally interdependent?"
- "How do we define diversity in our school? Are we addressing issues of diversity in meaningful ways?"

Representative Actions Demonstrating Emerging Knowledges for Standard 6

- Principals understand the organizational behavior of schooling and model effective strategies for change and collaboration.
- Principals value diversity and create capacities within the school community that invite diversity.
- The values, beliefs, and assumptions of school–community stakeholders are embraced with an awareness of the ethnicity and demographic characteristics (e.g., ethnicity, race, poverty, mobility, gender, etc.) unique to the school community. Policies and practices reflect this uniqueness.

Key Dispositions

A primary function of leadership is to build capacities that allow all educational stakeholders to reach their full potential. This cannot be accomplished unless an administrator clearly understands what he/she believes, values, and is committed to—a disposition imperative. When considering the political, social, economic, legal, and cultural contexts of leadership through a dispositional lens, asking the following questions may prove helpful:

- Can I easily articulate my beliefs, values, and assumptions regarding education?
- Do I clearly communicate my educational beliefs, values, and assumptions to stakeholders?
- Are my dispositions predictable and understood, or do they change depending on the situation and the stakeholder (i.e., Am I genuine?)?
- Do I solicit multiple sources of input from school–community stakeholders as a part of my leadership?
- Do my beliefs, values, and assumptions reflect the best interests of the educational common good or are they more individually focused?
- Do I build leadership capacity by investing in professional relationships? Do I define these relationships by trust, respect, and rapport?

Representative Comments Demonstrating Emerging Dispositions for Standard 6

- "In what ways are our school improvement activities aligned with district and state goals? In other words, are we all measuring success in similar ways?"
- "Do we really believe *all* students can learn?"
- "Mobility and poverty are barriers to student success in our school. In what ways can we ensure our students' families have capacities to support the education of their children?"
- "Although the students in our school have many immediate needs, we must prioritize these concerns to advocate successfully on their behalf."
- "What roles do parents have in our school improvement plan? How can we best engage them?"
- "If we truly value others, should we only ask questions we are prepared to hear the answers and be responsive to?"
- "What external forces are currently influencing our decisions regarding this policy? Should we be responsive to these forces?"
- "I realize you are unhappy with my decision regarding this discipline issue. I would like the opportunity to explain the due process procedure I used and the rationale I applied to the final decision."

Representative Actions Demonstrating Emerging Dispositions for Standard 6

- Principals join and are involved in professional memberships at the local, state, and national levels.
- Principals are active in developing legislative agendas for the professional organizations in which they are involved.
- Principals lead from a moral or value-laden perspective.
- Principals ensure the school's vision and mission are genuinely representative of the school community and use them to guide their leadership.
- Principals realign the expenditure of resources (e.g., time and money) with student outcomes that are supportive of the school's vision and mission.

Specific steps for building the portfolio are discussed in the next section. In addition, refer to the accompanying CD-ROM for further activities related to Standard 6.

Part 3: Portfolio Exercise for Standard 6

The following exercise will help students seeking administrative licensure to build their professional portfolio. Procedures are described here that will lead to a completed entry for a professional portfolio for Standard 6. A five-level scoring rubric to measure the level of standard attainment is contained in Appendix B. The rubric provides the rater with scoring criteria to evaluate the portfolio exercise.

1. Access your file box, the Standard 6 divider, and three manila folders.
2. Consider how you would promote success by understanding, responding to, and influencing the larger political, social, economic, legal, and cultural context as discussed in Chapter 6. Think about what activities a principal would use to demonstrate promoting success. Choose one activity that you will develop in your school setting. Examples include joining a professional organization for school leaders, facilitating a school improvement meeting with internal and external stakeholders, or meeting with policy makers at the local or state levels on issues of student advocacy. Think about the knowledges, performances, and dispositions associated with Standard 6 and discuss them in your narrative section.
3. Conduct the selected activity and keep a record through voice/video recorder, or word processing entry.
4. Review the record keeping and write a detailed reflection about what happened within the context of Standard 6. The reflection should include a description of the setting (e.g., place, time, participants, etc.), what happened and why, and what you would do differently if you had the opportunity and why.
5. Write about how the activity demonstrates your partial attainment of Standard 6.
6. Provide a written authenticity for the activity. For example, your principal writes a letter attesting to your performance of the activity, or an elected/appointed official tenders a letter of thanks for your service.
7. Place the videotape, audiotape, or electronic record in one folder. Place the reflections and authenticity evidence in the two remaining folders.
8. Carefully review all items and correct any errors.

A sample cover sheet and reflection narrative follow.

Sample Portfolio Entry

Standard 6: The Political, Social, Economic, Legal, and Cultural Context
Artifact: School improvement team meeting
October 19, 20XX
Jefferson High School
Mt. Vernon, VA

Artifact

During the beginning of the second semester I conducted a meeting of our school improvement team. The purpose of the meeting was to plan for our spring graduation ceremony. Feedback from staff and students had indicated that the ceremony had become outdated and did not reflect the growing diversity of our student population and their family values and cultures. During the previous summer, I had made a concerted effort to invite key community people to join our improvement team. My outreach included members of the Latino American community and our growing African American community. I was pleased that four people had accepted my invitation, three of whom were Hispanic Americans and one who was African American. In addition, I had sought out parents representing the same two cultures. Three parents joined the team—one African American and two Hispanic Americans. The rest of the team was comprised of four teachers and three students. The meeting was held in the principal's conference room adjacent to the school office. I have included a 30-minute unedited videotape of the meeting, which includes a discussion of how the ceremony can better reflect the values and culture of our diverse school population.

Reflection Narrative

I have become quite concerned about the growing gap between our mostly middle-class, white teaching staff and our increasingly diverse student population. Forty-two percent of our student body is Hispanic American and 23% is African American. The graduation ceremony was established in 1959 for a student population that was primarily of white descent. The ceremony has not changed in any way since then. The same music is played, the same expectations for dress are in place, and the comments from board members and school leaders have the same general message. It occurred to me that perhaps the Hispanic American students and the African American students may want to see the ceremony better reflect their cultures. I wasn't at all sure what this would mean, but I felt strongly that there should be discussion of the matter with the appropriate stakeholders. I opened the meeting by stating my thoughts just described herein. I then asked the group to form groups of two or three people, making sure that the groups were mixed regarding culture and ethnic background. Each group was charged with making three suggestions for how the ceremony could be changed. I explained that any ideas would be acceptable and that they had 20 minutes to complete their task. Following the groups' task, I asked each group to report their suggestions. I was pleased that there appeared to be little conflict about the various ideas. By the conclusion of the meeting we had agreed on three changes: music that represented diverse cultures, strict expectations of "Sunday" dress by students and parents, and conducting a concerted effort to encourage minority students to strive for class valedictorian. The team made plans to present the suggestions to the larger staff and receive their input. I am sure that there will be some kind of resistance to the changes, but with careful strategies, I believe the leaders of the staff will convince the others to support the changes. I look forward to working with the larger staff on the last

(continued)

BOX **6.1**   **Continued**

change—promoting minority representation for honors consideration at graduation. Traditionally, we have presented awards to white students. I need to plan carefully with the staff for how we can create opportunities for our minority students to receive these awards in the future.

Scoring Analysis for the Entry
Using the portfolio exercise scoring rubric (Appendix B), this entry would score a 3. The principal provided a clear explanation of the artifact, but could have been clearer about how the artifact shows an attainment of Standard 6. A stronger reflection would have mentioned key elements of the standard and explained how the artifact showed attainment of those elements.

Suggestions for Standard 6 Sample Artifacts
- A written analysis of a recent landmark case that has had an impact on how students or staff are treated
- A copy of the school's discipline manual showing adherence to legal regulations for students
- A videotape or audiotape of the candidate addressing a community group concerning a sensitive legal issue such as gangs, drugs, religion in schools, or textbook adoption
- A copy of a report to the superintendent or school board outlining the candidate's plan to address a particular politically sensitive issue such as district boundary changes, charter schools, state and national mandatory reform initiatives, or discipline policies
- A case study of a particular student with disabilities and how the candidate managed the student's progress while being sensitive to the student's legal rights

Part 4: Case Study, Standard 6

Read the scenario that follows and answer the questions at the end. Sample answers to each question are provided on the enclosed CD-ROM to guide you.

Nate Owens has just become the associate superintendent for curriculum and instruction in his district, following six years as a high school principal. He and his superintendent met last week with local state legislators to discuss their concerns about proposed changes in the state's high school graduation requirements. A significant percentage of the students served by Nate's district are the children of transient workers. Nate and many of his colleagues fear that the proposed changes will be so intimidating to many of their students that the dropout rate will increase as a result. He is anxious to find a compromise and would like the state to consider creating alternative pathways to achieve the results they desire. As a result of their discussion, one of the state legislators asked Nate to prepare a statement to be delivered at the state house of representatives to the full education committee.

> *Question 1:* What artifact, related to this activity, could Nate use to document his attainment of Standard 6, The Political, Social, Economic, Legal, and Cultural Context?
>
> *Question 2:* What knowledges, dispositions, and performances are demonstrated using the chosen artifact?

CHAPTER

7

Standards 7 and 8: Instructional Program and Policy Implementation

When there is a genuine vision (as opposed to the all-too-familiar "vision statement"), people excel and learn, not because they are told to, but because they want to.

—Senge, 1994, p. 9

A district administrator is an educational leader who guides, facilitates, and supports the success of all learners by providing leadership in curriculum development, learning assessment, instructional supervision, and program evaluation conducive to student learning, staff professional growth, and district accountability.

A district administrator is an educational leader who guides, facilitates, and supports the success of all learners by recommending and implementing policy that guides district operations.

OBJECTIVES

The learner will

- Understand the aspects of instructional leadership at the district level
- Understand the complex nature of policy development and implementation at the district level
- Practice the completion of portfolio entries for Standards 7 and 8
- Reflect on Standards 7 and 8 through interaction with case studies

Part 1: Examining Standards 7 and 8

When the Indiana Professional Standards Board charged an external school leaders committee with the task of recommending a standards-based, performance-assessed system of licensure for school administrators during the 1990s, two additional standards beyond those recommended by ISLLC emerged as a result of considering the uniqueness of district-level leadership (Indiana Professional Standards Board, 2004). Other states (e.g., Michigan) have identified their own unique standards-based outcomes not specifically manifested through an ISLLC standard. Because of the successful work Indiana has done with these unique standards for district-level leaders (i.e., superintendents and directors of curriculum, exceptional needs, and career and technical education), we suggest that educational administration stakeholders of other states consider implementing similar models as well. The reader might easily find these two additional standards embedded in the other ISLLC standards, but the pervasive expectation that district leaders provide instructional and policy leadership warrant their unique consideration. Although the additional standards specifically address district leadership, they have strong implications for building-level leadership as well.

Effective district-level leadership summons a unique array of knowledges, performances, and dispositions. The job description of the district administrator is complex, canvassing a broad educational landscape. Amidst the breadth and depth of district administration, the effective leader adopts a pedagogy immersed in two key areas: instructional leadership and policy leadership. Instructional leaders build capacities for effective teaching and learning in an *all-students* environment. Policy leaders not only recommend policy, but implement policy, enabling the district to reach its teaching and learning potential. Without a meaningful and persistent focus in these two key areas by district leaders, school improvement efforts and capacities that support effective teaching and learning are challenging to realize. Furthermore, meaningful and effective change initiatives throughout a district will be challenging to sustain without enabling policy support and a genuine instructional commitment to teaching and learning from district leadership.

Standard 7: Instructional Program

No single framework for district-level instructional leadership could adequately address the uniqueness of local schools and districts. Local variations must exist, depending on resources, district size, and instructional needs in general. Regardless of district-level position and unique local needs, six basic principles consistently permeate the instructional leader's district-level practice. These include building vision and mission capacity, supporting and sustaining change, fostering a collegial and collaborative environment, human resource administration, and questioning.

Building Vision and Mission Capacity

The district leader's first step toward becoming an instructional leader involves a thoughtful understanding of the mission and vision of the district and each school (Balch, 2003). Mission and vision statements are laden with values. District leaders must peel away the layers of meaning within these statements in search of core values. Once the values are understood and acknowledged, effective leaders articulate the difference between which values are currently practiced and which ones will hopefully be practiced in the future. The difference guides the district leader in planning.

Knowing who values and understands the mission and vision statements is essential. If vision and mission statements are not widely embraced by school–community stakeholders they will not reflect the culture and climate of the school. Such statements usually lack meaning and serve no practical purpose except for their symbolic presence. Effective district leaders focus on the core values of vision and mission statements, building capacities for the larger school community to codify and embrace them, and ensuring they are aligned with the climate and culture.

Effective district leaders recognize the power of vision and mission statements in reflecting a school and district's instructional identity. Without an instructional identity, it is difficult to articulate teaching and learning in the district, and educational purpose wanes. Furthermore, it is incumbent on district leaders to build capacities that ensure these identities are aligned. Otherwise, the district as a whole will lack a unique instructional identity.

An investment in exemplary building and district committees, focused on teaching and learning, strengthens vision and mission capacities. These committees are collaborative, diverse, include a variety of stakeholders, and have clear, well-defined charges. Instructional leaders provide time and other crucial resources for these committees to meet and engage in collaborative opportunities that strengthen and support the vision and mission statements, as well as align them districtwide.

Supporting and Sustaining Change

Instructional leadership from the district level includes a recognition and understanding of change as it relates to teaching and learning. Change is strongly correlated to improvement. Effective leaders can support and sustain change initiatives in meaningful and systemic ways that result in instructional improvement. Wholesale adoption of other schools' successes rarely yields positive results. Barth (1995) refers to this as "list logic." Effective instructional leaders understand change theory in relation to the unique needs of their schools and district. Tomlinson and Allan (2000) summarize nine fundamental change principles:

1. Change is imperative in today's classroom.
2. The focus of school change must be classroom practice.
3. For schools to become what they ought to be, systemic change is needed.
4. Change is difficult, slow, and uncertain.
5. Systemic change requires both leadership and administration.
6. To change schools, the culture of schools must change.
7. What leaders do speaks with greater force than what is said.
8. Change efforts need to link with a wider world.
9. Leaders for change have a results-based orientation.

A sound pedagogy of change for the district-level leader is immersed in these nine change principles.

Change is often "riddled with dilemmas, ambivalences, and paradoxes" (Fullan, 1991, p. 350). An effective district leader understands this, practicing patience and persistence. Most important, the district leader must model change and how to deal with the challenges of change initiatives. Modeling change can render leaders vulnerable because a roadmap for change does not exist and uncertainty looms over every change initiative. However, leaders who remain focused on the vision and mission of the schools and district can model focused and aligned change, consistent with improved teaching and learning.

Fostering a Collegial and Collaborative Environment

Strong instructional leaders value a collegial environment. Glatthorn (1997) notes that more effective schools have a climate characterized by collegiality. Collegiality (i.e., the equal empowerment of those sharing a common purpose) is enhanced when collaboration (i.e., working together effectively) is practiced. A collegial and collaborative environment should not be confused with a congenial (i.e., agreeable) environment. A congenial climate is nice and usually indicative of faculty and staff who enjoy gathering together to talk and discuss; however, congenial conversations are often not about the complex and difficult work of teaching and learning. It is easy to mistake a congenial conversation for collaborative and collegial conversations. Effective instructional leaders move beyond congenial relationships, striving for collaborative and collegial efforts focused on school improvement. These efforts are embedded in data-driven decisions, effective use of resources, diverse perspectives, alignment, and an *all-students* orientation.

When district leaders examine the breadth and depth of needed instructional leadership, it is easy to rush to in-service training and workshop opportunities as a means of providing leadership capacity. This kind of professional development has the advantage of delivering content quickly and is usually done so by experts in the content area. The challenge in relying on this instructional leadership capacity is minimizing disconnection between theory and practice. Often, what are needed are opportunities to dialogue and discuss a particular teaching/learning concept and develop a shared vision of what this would look and sound like (Gregory, 2003). Time, then, becomes a resource that effective instructional leaders learn to harness and utilize in meaningful ways for collaboration and collegiality.

Human Resource Administration

A frequently overlooked context of instructional leadership for district administrators is human resource administration and personnel selection. Hiring and retaining effective faculty and staff is central to effective teaching and learning. A district leader who truly understands the unique instructional needs that accompany any vacancy in a school or district is a leader who can hire an individual possessing the gifts and talents that are aligned with teaching and learning.

Barriers such as nepotism pressures or thin applicant pools often redefine personnel selection priorities, negating the importance of teaching and learning as a primary focus. This is compounded when searches for vacancies occur only when the need exists. Continuing this practice will not increase the applicant pool and encourages decision making that may not include instructional priorities. Effective instructional leaders build capacities for a systemic plan of recruitment that is specific to local needs (O'Laughlin, 2001).

Beyond a systemic recruitment plan, retention of effective faculty and staff should also be an instructional priority of the district leader. Although wages and wage-related benefits are a key consideration for retention, effective district leaders also address other important retention factors. These include, in part, professional development, enhanced responsibility, shared decision making, necessary resources, and a supportive climate and culture.

When district leaders consider the direct relationship between student achievement and educational personnel, an investment in a comprehensive system of recruitment and retention, unique to local needs, is a powerful contribution a district leader can make instructionally. The vision and mission of the school and district can only be realized when school personnel are willing and capable of doing so. Thus, recruitment and retention is central to teaching, learning, and the needs of *all students*.

Questioning

District leaders who are effective instructional leaders share a common attribute: They ask effective questions. Questioning is a powerful tool for seeking clarity and building capacities for improved teaching and learning. Furthermore, thoughtful questions seek deeper meaning and understanding. The single most important instructional question a district leader can ask of faculty, staff, and administration is, What is working and what is not? Be advised! Do not ask this question unless you are willing to listen and respond to the answer. For example, if a building principal responds to this powerful question with, "Study halls are no longer consistent with our school improvement goals. We simply don't have time for students to schedule a study hall, but I know they've been a long-standing tradition." Be prepared to respond. It is the imperative of the instructional leader and an opportunity to support challenging school improvement efforts. The effective instructional leader will likely encourage dialogue and discussion around the study hall issue, encouraging and supporting an action consistent with the vision and mission of the school, despite long-standing traditions.

Asking and listening to "why" and "how" questions will yield answers that are deeply rooted in motivation. It is generally accepted that motivation is an internal state or condition that activates and energizes behavior and gives it direction (Kleinginna & Kleinginna, 1981). Understanding the motivators that result in effective actions and behaviors regarding teaching and learning assists the instructional leader in helping a district attain its full achievement and improvement. Why are we collecting data? Why do we need more technology? How can we accomplish this for all students? Why did you decide to teach math? Why must I attend this meeting? These questions and their answers are deeply rooted in motivation.

Standard 8: Policy Implementation

The district administrator assumes a unique educational role by recommending and implementing policy. Policy is broadly defined as an adopted plan or course of action. Inherent to our system of educational governance is policy development and implementation. The National School Boards Association (2003) notes that "policies establish directions for the district; they set the goals, assign authority, and establish controls that make school governance and management possible. Policies are the means by which educators are accountable to the public" (p. 1). Garfield, Garfield, and Willardson (2003) acknowledge policy as an outcome of a political process with policy and politics inexorably tied together. Simply stated, policy provides education's foundation, and the district administrator ensures the foundation is sound. District administrators should consider four key constructs that frame policy leadership: policy roles and responsibilities, trust and control, professional memberships and affiliations, and the political environment.

Policy Roles and Responsibilities

From a policy role perspective, it must be acknowledged and understood that the district leader serves in a recommending and implementing capacity, whereas the school board serves in a policy-making capacity. Confusing these roles can create administrator–board conflict and tension. In 2001, the Institute for Educational Leadership published a report from their Task Force on School District Leadership. Although the task force acknowledged they lacked complete agreement on the problems and solutions of district leadership, they offered an insightful model that delineated the roles of the board as policy maker and the superintendent as administrator. It was termed the *policy governance model* and is illustrated by loosely defined arrangements or parameters used by successful districts. This model has strong implications for district leaders and suggests that school boards should

- Serve as the public's trustees and purchasing agents for education and assume accountability for superintendent and school system performance
- Collectively assert authority only as a full board, such that individual board member directives and requests are ignored
- Approach the superintendency as a position of chief executive officer, wielding exclusive authority over his or her staff and who is directly accountable for board expectations
- Authoritatively prescribe "ends" so that the superintendent or the public understand what is expected
- Provide the superintendent with the bounded freedom to prescribe "means" to reach board goals
- Define goals and limitations with specificity, yet using the broadest terms possible until board members can allow the superintendent full discretion within stated parameters
- Use school system performance against board criteria to evaluate the superintendent

In the absence of sound policy, political agendas can quickly emerge. Giles and Douglas (1990) found that conflicting political agendas between superintendents and their school boards was a major cause of involuntary turnovers, which included role disagreement. Similarly, the Public Agenda's study (2001) found that talented district administrators who leave the field are most likely to do so because of frustration with politics and bureaucracy (e.g., superintendents, 81%). Effective district leaders consistently recommend and implement policies that clearly define roles and responsibilities. In doing so, political agendas and the attendant conflicts are minimized.

Trust and Control

Effective district leaders understand the delicate balance trust and control play in policy administration. Because policy has the force of law, the authority of which is granted through state legislatures, only policy that is necessary to work within the laws and regulations of local, state, and federal governments, and to create opportunities for the **greater school community,** should be considered.

Excessive policy recommendation and implementation can be perceived as a lack of trust. For example, a district leader may have knowledge of a few teachers extending their spring vacations by using sick days. The effective administrator deals directly with these teachers and their building administrators to resolve the inappropriate use of sick days and avoids any temptation to recommend and implement a policy precluding such actions in the future. For the majority of faculty and staff who return from spring break on time, a new policy regarding the use of sick days could be interpreted as a clear message of distrust from district administration.

Excessive policy recommendation and implementation can also be perceived as an issue of control. No doubt complying with laws, regulations, and creating opportunities for local schools' greater educational communities will necessitate a comprehensive policy agenda, but unnecessary policy begs the question: Who is in control of teaching and learning at the district level? An overabundance of policy suggests that local board officials, and state and federal regulations, are scripting teaching and learning in a one-size-fits-all environment, leaving little control at the classroom level. Policies then become a means of compliance, wrought with politics.

It is no myth that federal, state, and local controls will leverage certain district policies that must be adopted and implemented, such as the No Child Left Behind Act enacted by President Bush in 2001. However, the teaching and learning capacities that exist in a complex and dynamic educational environment also necessitate leverage for control at the classroom level, where teaching and learning are most intimate. Effective leaders understand the many external and internal forces competing for control of teaching and learning, using this understanding to support educational capacities for success with a minimum of policy.

For example, policies and their attendant guidelines that are restatements of existing acts, laws, codes, or regulations are redundant and unnecessary. Because they were promulgated and exist elsewhere for educational purposes, to codify them at the local level serves no meaningful purpose. Furthermore, should these acts, laws, codes, or regulations change, the local policy must change too if full compliance is to be maintained. This alone could be a daunting task.

Professional Memberships and Affiliations

Effective policy leadership requires a current knowledge and understanding of existing and emerging policy. Professional memberships and affiliations can provide essential opportunities for policy currency just as it enhances instructional leadership. Membership and affiliations at all levels (i.e., local, regional, state, and national) ensure access to policy databases, policy guidance, publications, resources, policy services, membership directories, meetings, division membership (i.e., special interest groups such as rural, urban, superintendent, etc.), conferences, and workshops. District leaders who take advantage of professional membership and affiliation benefits can strengthen their policy leadership capacities for recommendation and implementation.

The Political Environment

Policy is immersed in a political environment, whether at the local, state, or national levels. Denying the politics of education limits policy leadership effectiveness. Garfield,

Garfield, and Willardson (2003) defines "politics" relating to educational policy as a natural phenomenon, occurring by virtue of social interactions, involving negotiating, networking, and strategizing to achieve specific goals. Dionne (1991) notes, "a nation that hates politics will not long survive as a democracy" (p. 355). The political context of education, by its very nature, is wrought with both conflict and collaboration. Although some acknowledge politics as the core of educational policy development, others dispute the very existence of politics in educational policy.

The contentious and controversial climate associated with politics and educational policy may have much to do with its values-laden influences. Controversy and contention is inevitable when, as Cooper, Fusarelli, and Randall (2004) suggest, "personal beliefs and values are raised to become public beliefs and values, which all are asked or forced to accept" (p. 157). The values that have generally surrounded political policy debate in the last decade include equity, excellence, efficiency, and choice (Sergiovanni, Bulingame, Coobs, & Thurston, 1992). In recent years, the values of adequacy and effectiveness have emerged as two additional values, an outgrowth of the nation's accountability movement. And, deeply embedded in education, equality has also influenced decades of policy and politics. These seven values are competing, in a sense, because trying to gain ground in one may mean to lose ground in another. Too much political reliance on any one of the seven values can manifest itself into detrimental policy for teaching and learning in an all-students environment, such as the years of the Great Society enacted by President Lyndon B. Johnson. Policy development, recommendation, and implementation best serve education when multiple values are considered.

A helpful lens with which to view policy distinguishes between student achievement inputs and outputs. Input policy includes language supportive of resources and reforms that builds a foundation for achievement capacities. On the other hand, output policy is characterized by its measurable, quantifiable language focused on achievement results. Although values are paired in many combinations, influencing both input and output policy, trends have emerged that can inform the district leader. A recent pedagogical shift is occurring that suggests output values (i.e., effectiveness, adequacy, and excellence), underpinned by our nation's expectation for accountability, have emerged as key values dramatically influencing educational policy at the state and national levels. Input values (i.e., equity, equality, and efficiency) continue to dominate local policy development and implementation. A strong historical precedent of input values at the state and federal levels consistently influences local policy as well. The value of choice is currently enjoying a strong presence at every political–policy level in both input and output policy. This is due in part to the fact that, as a nation of consumers influenced by market forces, individual choice permeates our culture. This value now profoundly influences education as well.

These seven persistent and pervasive values might be defined as follows:

1. Equality—Sameness
2. Equity—Fairness
3. Efficiency—minimal waste and highly effective
4. Choice—Alternatives
5. Excellence—Quality achievement
6. Effective—Achieving desired results
7. Adequacy—Sufficient to satisfy requirements

The wise district leader understands the competing nature of these values and can distinguish between input and output values. Furthermore, it must be understood that state and local differences will dictate the appropriate combinations of values to provide essential policy leadership for teaching and learning.

Part 2: Key Performances, Knowledges, and Dispositions for Standard 7

Key Performances

Part 1 of this chapter provided a conceptual context for instructional leadership. Performances apply these contexts to authentic practice. The five succeeding performances are of primary instructional importance. It is the district leader who must build instructional capacities for teaching and learning to flourish.

Performances
A district administrator facilitates processes and engages in activities that

1. Establish curriculum and instructional strategies to meet the needs of a diverse school community and its learners
2. Align curriculum with appropriate levels of learner development and styles
3. Involve appropriate faculty and community members in decision making regarding curriculum and special programs
4. Evaluate the use of resources, including technology, for effectiveness, equability, and relevance to the instructional process
5. Use test results and other assessments appropriately to improve the educational system

Representative Comments Demonstrating Emerging Performances for Standard 7

- "If we are to invest in portable technology, how will it make a difference in achieving our instructional and learning goals?"
- "What additional assessments do we need beyond the state assessments to enhance and inform our instructional efforts?"
- "If we know our highly mobile students' families leave and return during the same academic year, how can minimize this challenge to ensure student success?"
- "In what ways can we evidence that what the state is testing is what is being taught?"
- "In what ways are our inclusive practices for special populations ensuring that grade-level expectations are being met?"

Representative Actions Demonstrating Emerging Performances for Standard 7

- The district administrator provides resource support for a broad range of professional development opportunities tied to school improvement processes and learning goals/objectives.

- The district administrator encourages committee structures at the building and district levels that are inclusive of external stakeholders, to enhance teaching and learning practices.
- The district administrator advocates for the diverse needs of learners and supports the adequacy of resources needed by seeking external funding mechanisms.
- The building administrator supports and furthers a systemic recruitment plan rather than a wait-and-see approach to vacancies to ensure depth in the instructional recruitment pool, yielding quality faculty and staff.
- The building administrator grounds decision making in the district and building vision and mission statements to model the importance of outcomes-based leadership.

Key Knowledges and Dispositions

Previously this chapter demonstrated how an effective administrator will use the performances associated with Standard 7 to develop instructional leadership. In addition to performances, Standard 7 contains knowledges and dispositions. This section will assist the administrator in understanding behaviors that demonstrate attainment of the knowledges and dispositions. The following lists detail the key knowledges and dispositions from Standard 7:

Knowledges
A district administrator has knowledge and understanding of

1. Development of core curriculum design and delivery systems for diverse school communities
2. Instructional taxonomies, goals, objectives, and processes
3. Current trends and future learning needs
4. Curricular alignment to improve student performance and higher order thinking
5. The development, implementation, and monitoring of change processes to improve learning and climates for learning
6. Appropriate teaching methods and assessment strategies
7. Testing and alternative methods of assessment to evaluate learner achievement
8. A variety of instructional strategies based on current research
9. Student achievement monitoring and reporting systems
10. Diverse learner needs

Dispositions
A district administrator believes in, values, and is committed to

1. Developing and implementing a core curriculum design with instructional strategies that reflect multicultural sensitivity and multiple learning styles
2. Using technology appropriately to enhance educational programming
3. Maintaining communication regarding curriculum among developmental levels and content areas
4. Using multiple assessment tools in determining the effectiveness of educational programs

5. Using multiple information sources for gathering perspectives from the educational community

Key Knowledges

Considering the comprehensive knowledges associated with instructional leadership, district leaders must choose how they will spend their time. Armed with comprehensive instructional knowledge, district leaders can conduct themselves in symbolic and substantive ways that infuse instructional leadership values and purpose into the teaching and learning process. However, an instructional knowledge base is necessary.

Representative Comments Demonstrating Emerging Knowledges for Standard 7

- "How can we ensure our local assessments are both valid and reliable?"
- "Although the global assessment data are encouraging, what does the disaggregated data tell us about our learners by gender, race, ethnicity, or poverty level?"
- "What 'best practices' are we currently using and how do we know if they are effective?"
- "In what ways are we assessing what is working and what is not?"
- "Is there evidence to support the 'written' curriculum is the 'taught' curriculum?"

Representative Actions Demonstrating Emerging Knowledges for Standard 7

- The district administrator ensures student achievement is disaggregated sufficiently to be understood, valued, and acted on at the building and classroom levels.
- The district administrator advocates for "adequate" resources to meet diverse learner needs.
- The district administrator understands the professional development resource investment (e.g., time and money) necessary to promote collaborative discussion/dialogue through meetings, advisories, or other forums that lead to the aligned instructional outcomes for all learners.
- The district administrator values a variety of means to develop curriculum and deliver instruction, resisting one-size-fits-all approaches.
- The district administrator seeks and supports teacher leadership as a means of strengthening school improvement initiatives.

Key Dispositions

For district leaders, ordinary routines are power indicators of instructional leadership. Ask yourself the following representative questions that assist in defining your instructional dispositions:

- Do you regularly visit schools and classrooms?
- Do you attend or facilitate meetings dealing with instructional programming?
- Do you frequently refer to the mission and vision statements to guide decision making?
- Do you engage in professional development opportunities regarding teaching and learning, and encourage the same of your building administrators?

- Do you model coaching, facilitation, and collaboration?
- Do you attend in-service opportunities and remain for the entire session to model active learning?

Representative Comments Demonstrating Emerging Dispositions for Standard 7

- "I know this is important to your school, but how does it align with the goals of the district and state?"
- "In what ways are we ensuring equity and equality in the transition from elementary school to middle school for all learners, regardless of the elementary school from which they come?"
- "How do the capital requests for technology for your building align with the five-year technology plan our district has created?"
- "Our shift from inputs to outputs is a shift from teaching to learning. Do our school improvement plans focus on inputs or outputs?"

Representative Actions Demonstrating Emerging Dispositions for Standard 7

- The district administrator challenges each school to articulate its instructional identity (i.e., What do you stand for?).
- The district administrator models collaboration and embraces the outcomes of empowered committees.
- The district administrator is sensitive to change and understands the often slow pace of change.
- The district administrator advocates for a sound instructional identity by asking clarifying "how" and "why" questions.

Specific steps for building the portfolio are discussed in the next section. In addition, refer to the accompanying CD-ROM for further activities related to Standard 7.

Part 3: Portfolio Exercise for Standard 7

The following exercise will help individuals seeking administrative licensure to build their professional portfolios. Procedures are described here that will lead to a completed entry for a professional portfolio for Standard 7.

1. Access your file box, the Standard 7 divider, and three manila folders.
2. Consider how you would promote success by building vision and mission capacity, supporting and sustaining change, fostering a collegial and collaborative environment, hiring and retaining effective faculty, and asking thoughtful questions, as discussed in Chapter 7. Within this conceptual framework, think about what activities a district administrator would use to provide leadership in curriculum development, learning assessment, instructional supervision, and program evaluation conducive to student learning, staff professional growth, and district accountability. Choose one activity that you will develop in your school district. Examples include providing

leadership in moving from a junior high to middle school configuration within the school district, evaluating the effectiveness of block scheduling, or providing professional development opportunities to assist principals with implementing their school improvement plans. Think about the knowledges, performances, and dispositions associated with Standard 7, and discuss them in your narrative section.

3. Conduct the activity you select and keep a record of how it was enacted (videotape, tape recorder, journal entries, etc.).

4. Once the activity is complete, review your video, audio, or written record and reflect on what happened and how it relates to Standard 7. The reflection should include a narrative description of what you did, who was involved, when it occurred, and the outcome. Upon reflection, what would you do differently if you had the opportunity to perform the activity again?

5. Discuss how the activity shows partial attainment of Standard 7.

6. Provide a written authenticity for the activity. For example, your superintendent or a school board member writes a letter attesting to your performance of the activity.

7. Place the videotape, audiotape, or artifact in one folder. Place the reflections and authenticity evidence in the two remaining folders.

8. Carefully review all items and correct any errors. Have a friend or colleague proofread your materials to find any errors you may have missed.

A sample cover sheet and reflection narrative follow.

BOX **7.1**

Sample Portfolio Entry

Artifact for Standard 7: Instructional Program

Names of Artifact: Curriculum alignment charts

Date: April 7, 20XX

Shawnee County School District

Artifact:
The attached charts provide documentation that the K–12 curriculum for the Shawnee County Schools is aligned with state standards.

Reflection Narrative
Last fall the state of XXXX adopted new standards for student achievement in English language arts, mathematics, and science. To ensure that the curricula and instructional programs for the Shawnee County School District are appropriately aligned with these revised standards, I convened a series of meetings during the past several months. The subject area teams (SATs) for each of these three areas met regularly, under my leadership, to analyze our curricula and programs. Each SAT is comprised of one teacher representative for each grade K–12, one elementary and one secondary building administrator, one media specialist, three parent representatives, and a content-area faculty representative from a local university. The teams were asked to examine textbooks,

(continued)

BOX **7.1**   **Continued**

technology, course outlines, assessment tools, and all supplementary materials to verify that the standards are being addressed appropriately. The charts show the result of these analyses.

During the process, the teams and I made note of any standards that did not appear to be adequately covered in the curricula. After analyzing these notes, I have decided to appoint grade-level or course-specific subcommittees of each SAT. The role of these subcommittees will be to submit recommendations for the revision of the curriculum to ensure that all state standards are being addressed.

As I consider the task of curriculum review undertaken by these teams, I perceive a need to establish such SATs in all areas of our curriculum. I need to plan time for each team to meet annually to review and revise our curriculum. I plan to establish these teams before the end of the current school year. In the fall, I will bring together all the SATs for a professional development workshop. This workshop will include a review of various instructional taxonomies and learning theories as well as an introduction to current trends. The SATs will receive specific training in the application of curriculum review models. The establishment of these SATs will result in an annual review of all curricula that will improve district accountability and identify areas in which additional staff professional development is needed. The ultimate outcome will be improved instruction resulting in greater student learning.

Scoring Analysis for the Entry
Using the portfolio exercise scoring rubric (Appendix B), this entry would score a 5. One strength of this entry is in the choice of artifact/event. There is clear evidence that the superintendent is developing a meaningful, long-term plan for the improvement of the schools, and that the plan will impact the knowledge and practice of education professionals in the district. The analysis and reflection demonstrate the writer's grasp of the future implications of the activities. This entry shows compelling evidence of consistent efforts to attain Standard 7.

Part 4: Case Study, Standard 7

Read the scenario that follows and answer the questions at the end. Sample answers to each question are provided on the enclosed CD-ROM to guide you.

Ana Padilla is the superintendent of a suburban school district that serves about 8000 students. The district includes 11 elementary schools, three middle schools, and one high school. The district is located in a southwestern community. Many people in the community espouse traditional conservative philosophies, although the local college attracts a population that adopts more liberal philosophies. Several months ago a group of high school students presented Ana with a petition requesting that creationism be taught along with evolution theory in the high school biology courses. State standards are ambiguous about the inclusion of creation theory in the science curriculum. The teachers in the science department at the high school are opposed to the inclusion of creation theory in the biology courses. Ana was impressed by the serious and thoughtful presentation of the students. She also respects the professionalism of the biology teachers. Ana has done some research to learn how other districts handle controversial topics. After giving the matter careful consideration, she decided to approach the social studies department with a proposal for the development of a new course. The course would focus on problem-solving strategies and the consideration of diverse viewpoints through the examination of various topics and current issues of interest to the students. The chair of the social studies department reacted with interest to this idea, and is willing to work with Ana to develop a proposed course outline.

Question 1: What artifacts related to this activity could Ana use to demonstrate that she has met Standard 7, Instructional Program? Defend the choice of these artifacts by explaining how they illustrate the knowledges, dispositions, and performances that exemplify this standard.

Question 2: Using the artifacts you selected in question 1, write a sample portfolio entry to describe, analyze, and reflect on Ana's attainment of Standard 7 as evidenced by this activity.

Question 3: Apply the scoring rubric found in Appendix B to evaluate the first draft of your answer to question 2. Based on your application of the rubric, revise your sample entry. Describe why you made your revisions and explain how the changes strengthen the validity of your entry.

Part 5: Key Performances Knowledges, and Dispositions for Standard 8

Key Performances

Part 1 of this chapter provided a conceptual context for policy implementation. Performances apply these contexts to authentic practice. The four succeeding performances form the foundation of a district leader's policy perspective. It is the district leader who fosters a policy focus for elected/appointed officials, faculty, staff and administration, and the larger school community. This long-standing perspective can be found in decades-old leadership handbooks for district leaders (e.g., Reeder, 1944).

Performances
A district administrator facilitates processes and engages in activities that

1. Maintain compliance with state, federal, and local laws and regulations
2. Promote positive relationships with the school board
3. Keep all staff current on applicable laws and regulations
4. Communicate all policies to staff and make them available to the greater school community

Representative Comments Demonstrating Emerging Performances for Standard 8

- "I'm glad you are interested in attending the law conference. I'll add 'legal updates' to next month's administrative council meeting so you can share what you learned with the other administrators."

- "Let's travel to the school board conference together. It will give all of us an opportunity to talk informally."
- "Please ensure the policy updates are shared with everyone who maintains a policy handbook according to the checklist, including the public libraries."

Representative Actions Demonstrating Emerging Performances for Standard 8

- The district administrator develops and supports a policy revision plan to maintain local, state, and federal compliance.
- The district administrator values "trust" as an essential characteristic of effective superintendent–board relationships.
- The district administrator ensures a plan is developed and supported to share critical information among faculty and staff.

Key Knowledges and Dispositions

Previously this chapter demonstrated how an effective administrator will use the performances associated with Standard 8 to implement policy. In addition to performances, Standard 8 contains knowledges and dispositions. This section will assist the administrator in understanding behaviors that demonstrate attainment of the knowledges and dispositions. The following lists detail the key knowledges and dispositions from Standard 8:

Knowledges
A district administrator has knowledge and understanding of

1. The system of public school governance in our democracy
2. The dynamics of superintendent–board of education roles and relationships
3. Conflict resolution skills
4. How to formulate sound district policy
5. Adapting local policy to accommodate state and federal regulations and requirements
6. Procedures to avoid civil and criminal liabilities
7. The contributions and benefits of professional organizations

Dispositions
A district administrator believes in, values, and is committed to

1. Working within the laws and regulations of state, federal, and local governments
2. Supporting the current fundamental system of the school system
3. Creating educational opportunities for the greater school community

Key Knowledges

The knowledges associated with policy implementation provide the link between the district leader's unilateral actions and the complex dimensions of education. The alchemy of educational policy transmuted into district effectiveness and educational opportunity for *all* is achieved when the district leader garners the policy knowledge necessary for thoughtful development, implementation, and enforcement.

Representative Comments Demonstrating Emerging Knowledges for Standard 8

- "My board of trustees will not be surprised; communication is of the utmost importance."
- "Involvement in professional organizations is an excellent means of reducing the isolation inherent to district leadership and developing critical networks for problem solving."
- "Please share the essential components of this harassment risk management plan with faculty and staff this fall; it is an excellent prevention and awareness tool."
- "Before approving the final reading of this policy, I wanted to assure members of the board that this policy has been fully discussed with building stakeholders."
- "Although the legislative bill was not passed into law, we should be encouraged that the level of awareness has been raised regarding this topic and it will no doubt emerge again as an item of legislative educational interest."

Representative Actions Demonstrating Emerging Knowledges for Standard 8

- The district administrator fully discloses information to avoid manipulation and to ensure a democratic process.
- The superintendent ensures the roles and responsibilities of elected/appointed board members and district administrators are clearly articulated and understood.
- The district administrator values the federalist nature of public education, respecting a state's constitutional charge to provide an education, even when competing with issues of local control.
- The district administrator takes time daily to be visible throughout the school community, utilizing multiple means of communication with internal and external stakeholders.
- The district administrator values cooperation above competition, understanding that for-profit principles do not seamlessly align with the not-for-profit educational sector.

Key Dispositions

As district leaders assume a burgeoning roll in policy implementation at the state, federal, and local levels of government, they must demonstrate a belief, value, and commitment to sound educational policy at all levels. Beyond implementation, this means demonstrating involvement in policy discourse and communicating policy understanding to school–community stakeholders.

Representative Comments Demonstrating Emerging Dispositions for Standard 8

- "Although the tests are high-stakes assessments, we must not settle for any unethical means to raise our test scores. Teaching and learning are far too important to be reduced to 'quick-fix' schemes."
- "I realize that income and sales tax increases may seem unpopular, but until more stable means of wealth are identified, it is the most 'progressive' way to reduce local property taxes."

- "Given the number of school families whose language is not primarily English, how might the schools assist in creating learning opportunities for the families of our students?"

Representative Actions Demonstrating Emerging Dispositions for Standard 8

- District administrators value an ethical leadership pedagogy, knowing that their personal and professional choices reflect on their districts.
- District administrators advocate for lifelong learning, finding teaching/learning opportunities for internal and external stakeholders of all ages.
- District administrators maintain legal currency through active organizational membership, conference/seminar attendance, and active networking.

Specific steps for building the portfolio are discussed in the next section. In addition, refer to the accompanying CD-ROM for further activities related to Standard 8.

Part 6: Portfolio Exercise for Standard 8

The following exercise will help individuals seeking administrative licensure to build their professional portfolios. Procedures are described here that will lead to a completed entry for a professional portfolio for Standard 8. A five-level scoring rubric to measure the level of standard attainment is contained in Appendix B. The rubric provides the rater with scoring criteria to evaluate the portfolio exercise.

1. Access your file box, the Standard 8 divider, and three manila folders.
2. Consider how you would promote success of all learners by recommending and implementing policies that guide district operations, as discussed in Chapter 7. Using four key constructs presented in Chapter 7, think about what activities a district administrator would use to provide policy leadership. Choose one activity that you will develop in your school district. Examples include working with the school board on implementing a teacher recruitment and retention policy; working with principals, parents, and students on implementation of a recently approved student rights policy; or collaborating with local government officials on jointly funding and implementing an after-school program for at-risk students. Think about the knowledges, performances, and dispositions associated with Standard 8 and discuss them in your narrative section.
3. Conduct the activity you select and keep a record of how it was enacted (videotape, tape recorder, journal entries, etc.).
4. Once the activity is complete, review your video, audio, or written record and reflect on what happened and how it relates to Standard 8. The reflection should include a narrative description of what you did, who was involved, when it occurred, and the outcome. Upon reflection, what would you do differently if you had the opportunity to perform the activity again?
5. Discuss how the activity shows partial attainment of Standard 8.

6. Provide a written authenticity for the activity. For example, your superintendent or a school board member writes a letter attesting to your performance of the activity.
7. Place the videotape, audiotape, or electronic medium in one folder. Place the reflections and authenticity evidence in the two remaining folders.
8. Carefully review all items and correct any errors. Have a friend or colleague proofread your materials to find any errors you may have missed.

A sample cover sheet and reflection narrative follow.

BOX **7.2**

Sample Portfolio Entry

Artifact for Standard 8: Policy Implementation

Names of Artifacts: agendas, announcement of public meetings to discuss new state testing program

Date: September, 20XX

Chesterfield Township Schools

Artifacts

These agendas document a series of meetings I conducted with parents and staff to explain the ramifications of the new statewide testing program to be implemented this year.

Reflection Narrative

There has been a great deal of media coverage recently about the state's newly adopted testing program, yet that coverage has been greatly lacking in details about the specifics of the program. At the beginning of this school year, I attended a staff meeting at each building in my district. I spoke with teachers and principals about the legislation and its impact on our district. In addition to sharing information about the requirements of the new law, I provided staff with a timetable to explain when the tests will be administered. I also explained the criteria the state will use to evaluate the performance of our schools. During question-and-answer sessions, I addressed teachers' specific concerns and clarified their understanding of the new law.

As a follow-up to the staff meetings, I spoke at a meeting of the school council for each building. (The dates, times, and locations of these public meetings were widely advertised. If parents were unable to attend a meeting at their child's school, they were encouraged to attend a meeting at another site. Other interested members of the community were also invited to attend.) During these meetings I focused on explaining what the new law says, how our schools will apply the new testing program, and what impact it will have on the students. Again, question-and-answer sessions allowed me to address the specific concerns of the parents.

The value in holding these meetings was the opportunity it provided me to ensure that everyone received consistent information about the new law. I met with staff members first to be certain they would be able to speak knowledgeably to parents and community members who might hesitate to approach me with questions. Both the staff and community meetings proved useful in disseminating this information. In retrospect, I believe I should have created handouts for distribution at these meetings to highlight the important features of the legislation and the ways in which

(continued)

BOX **7.2**   **Continued**

it will impact our students. These could have been useful tools in helping the public, in particular, understand the new law. They may forget the details of the law by the time test scores are reported next spring. To compensate for this oversight, I plan to develop a handout to be sent to parents with the test results when they are distributed.

Scoring Analysis for the Entry
Using the portfolio exercise scoring rubric (Appendix B), this is a level 5 entry. The superintendent clearly describes consistent efforts to attain Standard 8, Policy Implementation, through demonstrated efforts to communicate policy to the staff and the greater school community. The analysis and reflection highlight both the strengths and weaknesses of the event, and a specific action is identified for the future.

Part 7: Case Study, Standard 8

Read the scenario that follows and answer the questions at the end. Sample answers to each question are provided on the enclosed CD-ROM to guide you.

John Alexander is the superintendent of a district experiencing a severe financial crisis. Like other districts in his state, his schools are receiving less funding than they had anticipated due to a state budget shortfall. Rising employee health care costs and increasing utility prices are compounding the problem. John has asked the school board to support his request for a referendum to increase local taxes in support of the schools. One member of the board, a retired building contractor, is adamantly opposed to raising taxes for any reason. He has the support of a vocal group of senior citizens who feel they should not be taxed to support the schools when they do not have children who attend those schools. This outspoken board member has verbally attacked John at public board meetings. The media also printed the board members' unofficial comments, suggesting the superintendent is "an excessive spender lacking any understanding of the problems of seniors living on a fixed income." The rest of the board agrees with John that the proposed referendum could help prevent further financial problems in the district, but they do not receive the same attention from the media. John is planning a public relations campaign to counteract the negative press the referendum has been receiving. He is rallying teachers and parents to write letters to the editor in support of the referendum. He plans to appear on local news/interview programs on both radio and television stations. During these appearances, he plans to discuss what programs and staff positions will have to be eliminated if the referendum fails, as well as what programs and services the district will be able to maintain or add if the referendum passes. John is also asking supportive community members to donate funds to purchase billboard space and make yard signs with the slogans "Vote Yes For Our Children" and "Better Schools Make a Better Community For Everyone."

Question 1: Is this problem/activity/event a good choice for John to make for his portfolio entry for Standard 8, Policy Implementation? Why or why not? What performances, knowledges, and dispositions related to Standard 8 could John document using this project? Be specific.

Question 2: What artifacts related to this activity could John use to demonstrate that he has met Standard 8, Policy Implementation? Defend the choice of these artifacts by explaining how they illustrate the knowledges, dispositions, and performances that exemplify this standard.

Question 3: Using the artifacts you selected in question 1, write a sample portfolio entry to describe, analyze, and reflect on John's attainment of Standard 8 as evidenced by this activity.

Question 4: Apply the scoring rubric found in Appendix B to evaluate the first draft of your answer to question 3. Based on your application of the rubric, revise your sample entry. Describe why you made your revisions and explain how the changes strengthen the validity of your entry.

GLOSSARY

The following terms may have special meaning when used in the recommended standards:

Assessment   The systematic collection of data pertaining to programs or people

Best practice   The continuous process of learning, feedback, reflection, and analysis of what works, what does not work, and why

Collaboration   To work together in a joint intellectual effort

Consensus   A general agreement among a group of people; everyone does not have to accept the idea, 100%, but at the very least, almost everyone can live with it

Cost benefit analysis   A management concept based on a model of efficiency that uses measurable inputs and outputs (e.g., expenditures and test scores) for decision making

Diversity   Recognizing that every person is made up of distinctly different characteristics, qualities, and elements

Equity   The state, quality, or ideal of being just, impartial, and fair; allows for people of all genders, ethnicities, races, and creeds to have equal opportunities

Greater school community   Includes everyone in the school and the community

Leadership   Having the capacity to lead; possessing the knowledges, skills, and dispositions necessary to lead effectively

Mission   A statement created by a body or organization describing that group's overarching inner calling to pursue an activity or perform a service; a roadmap to the vision

School climate   A term referring to the extent to which a school is characterized by effective teaching and learning, quality leadership, and a values-laden environment

School culture   The habits, beliefs, skills, and behaviors exhibited in a school

School community   All those directly associated with a school, including students, parents, teachers, administrators, secretaries, custodians, cooks, bus drivers, etc.

Stakeholders   All persons who have an interest in what goes on in a school, including students, parents, teachers, bus drivers, custodians, cooks, administrators, secretaries, and people not directly associated with the school but who live in the community, such as business leaders, senior citizens, and adults who no longer have children in school

Standards   Descriptive of a degree of requirement, excellence, or attainment; provide guidelines for what is or should be an effective educator or administrator

Vision   A statement of the current goals of a body or organization; descriptive of what is to be pursued or achieved within a specified period of time; the "dream"

The Standards

Standard 1: A Vision of Learning

A school administrator is an educational leader who promotes the success of all students by facilitating the development, articulation, implementation, and stewardship of a vision of learning that is shared and supported by the greater school community.

Performances
The administrator facilitates processes and engages in activities to ensure that

1. The vision, mission, and goals of the school are effectively communicated to staff, parents, students, and community members
2. The core beliefs of the school are modeled for all stakeholders
3. The vision is developed with and among stakeholders
4. The contributions of school community members to the realization of the vision are celebrated
5. Progress toward the vision and mission is communicated to all stakeholders
6. The greater school community is involved in school improvement efforts
7. The vision shapes the educational programs, plans, and actions
8. An implementation plan is developed in which objectives and strategies to achieve the vision and goals are clearly articulated
9. Data related to student learning are used to develop the school vision and goals
10. Relevant demographic data pertaining to students and their families are used in developing the school mission and goals
11. Barriers to achieving the vision are identified, clarified, and addressed
12. Resources are sought to support the implementation of the school mission and goals
13. The vision, mission, and implementation plans are regularly monitored, evaluated, and revised

Knowledges
The administrator has a knowledge and understanding of

1. Learning goals in a pluralistic society
2. The principles of developing and implementing strategic plans
3. Theories of educational leadership (e.g., the categories of systems theory, change theory, and motivational theory)
4. Information sources, data collection, and data analysis strategies
5. Effective communication (e.g., writing, speaking, listening, use of technology)
6. Negotiation skills for consensus building
7. The foundations of education

Dispositions
The administrator believes in, values, and is committed to

1. The educability of all
2. The ideal of the common good
3. A school vision of high standards of learning
4. Continuous school improvement
5. Providing the opportunity for inclusion of all stakeholders in the school community
6. Ensuring that students have the knowledge, skills, and values needed to become successful adults
7. A willingness to examine continuously one's own assumptions, beliefs, and practices
8. The work ethic required for high levels of personal and organizational performance

Standard 2: School Culture and Instructional Program

A school administrator is an educational leader who promotes the success of all students and staff by advocating, nurturing, and sustaining a school culture and instructional program conducive to student learning and staff professional growth.

Performances
The administrator facilitates processes and engages in activities to ensure that

1. All individuals are treated with fairness, dignity, and respect
2. Professional development promotes a focus on student learning consistent with the school vision and goals
3. There is a culture of high expectations for self, student, and staff performance
4. The responsibilities of all are defined
5. Student and staff accomplishments are recognized and celebrated
6. Barriers to student learning are identified, clarified, and addressed
7. Diversity is considered in developing learning experiences
8. Lifelong learning is encouraged and modeled
9. Multiple opportunities to learn are available to all students and staff
10. The school is organized and aligned for success
11. Curricular, cocurricular, and extracurricular programs are designed, implemented, evaluated, and refined
12. Curriculum decisions are based on research, expertise of teachers, the recommendations of learned societies, and the needs of the community
13. The school culture and climate are assessed on a regular basis
14. A variety of sources of information are used to make decisions
15. Student learning is assessed using a variety of techniques
16. Multiple sources of information regarding performance are used by staff and students
17. A variety of supervisory models is employed
18. Student guidance programs are developed to meet the needs of students and their families

19. Technologies are used for teaching and learning
20. Data from pure research are used in decision making

Knowledges
The administrator has a knowledge and understanding of

1. School cultures
2. Student growth and development
3. Applied learning theories
4. Applied motivational theories
5. Curriculum design, implementation, evaluation, and refinement
6. Principles of effective instruction
7. Measurement, evaluation, and assessment strategies
8. Diversity and its meaning for educational programs
9. Adult learning and professional development models
10. The change process for systems, organizations, and individuals
11. The role of technology in promoting student learning and professional growth

Dispositions
The administrator believes in, values, and is committed to

1. Student learning as the fundamental purpose of schooling
2. The proposition that all students can learn
3. The proposition that students learn in a variety of ways
4. Lifelong learning for self and others
5. Professional development as an integral part of school improvement
6. A safe and supportive learning environment
7. Preparing students to be contributing members of society

Standard 3: Management

A school administrator is an educational leader who promotes the success of all students and staff by ensuring management of the organization, operations, and resources for a safe, efficient, and effective learning environment.

Performances
The administrator facilitates processes and engages in activities to ensure that

1. Knowledge of learning, teaching, and student development is used in reaching management decisions
2. Operational procedures are designed and managed to maximize opportunities for successful learning
3. Emerging trends are recognized, studied, and applied as appropriate
4. Operational plans and procedures to achieve the vision and goals of the school are in place
5. Collective bargaining and other contractual agreements related to the school are effectively managed

6. The school plant, equipment, and support systems operate safely, efficiently, and effectively
7. Time is managed to maximize attainment of organizational goals
8. Potential problems and opportunities are identified
9. Problems are confronted and resolved in a timely manner
10. Financial, human, and material resources are aligned to the goals of the schools
11. The school acts entrepreneurially to support continuous improvement
12. Organizational systems are regularly monitored and modified as needed
13. Stakeholders are involved in decisions affecting schools
14. Responsibility is shared to maximize ownership and accountability
15. Effective problem-framing and problem-solving skills are used
16. Conflict is effectively managed
17. Effective group process and consensus-building skills are used
18. Effective communication skills are used
19. There is effective use of technology to manage school operations
20. Fiscal resources of the school are managed responsibly, efficiently, and effectively
21. A safe, clean, and aesthetically pleasing school environment is created and maintained
22. Confidentiality and privacy of school records are maintained

Knowledges
The administrator has a knowledge and understanding of

1. Theories and models of organizations, and the principles of organizational development
2. Human resources management and development
3. Operational policies and procedures at the school and district levels
4. Principles and issues relating to school safety and security
5. Principles and issues relating to fiscal operations of school management
6. Principles and issues relating to school facilities and use of space
7. Legal issues impacting school operations
8. Current technologies that support management functions

Dispositions
The administrator believes in, values, and is committed to

1. Making management decisions to enhance learning and teaching
2. Accepting responsibility
3. High-quality standards, expectations, and performances
4. Involving stakeholders in management processes
5. Cultivating a safe and trusting environment

Standard 4: Collaboration with Families and the Community

A school administrator is an educational leader who promotes the success of all students by collaborating with families and community members, responding to diverse community interests and needs, and mobilizing community resources.

Performances
The administrator facilitates processes and engages in activities to ensure that

1. High visibility, active involvement, and communication with the larger community occur
2. Relationships with community leaders are established and nurtured
3. Respect is given to individuals and groups whose values, opinions, and cultures may conflict
4. Information about family and community concerns, expectations, and needs is used regularly
5. There is outreach to different business, religious, political, and service agencies and organizations
6. The school and community serve one another as resources
7. Available community resources are secured to help the school solve problems and achieve goals
8. Partnerships are established with area businesses, institutions of higher education, and community groups to strengthen programs and support school goals
9. Community stakeholders are treated equitably
10. Effective media relations are developed and maintained
11. A comprehensive program of community relations is established
12. Public resources and funds are used appropriately and wisely
13. Community collaboration is modeled for staff
14. Opportunities for staff to develop collaborative skills are provided
15. Multicultural awareness, gender sensitivity, and racial and ethnic appreciation are promoted

Knowledges
The administrator has a knowledge and understanding of

1. Emerging issues and trends that potentially impact the school community
2. The conditions and dynamics of the diverse school community (e.g., social, cultural, leadership, historical, and political)
3. Community resources (e.g., parental, business, governmental agencies, community, and social services)
4. Community relations and marketing strategies and processes
5. Successful models of school, family, business, community, government, and higher education partnerships
6. Community and district power structures

Dispositions
The administrator believes in, values, and is committed to

1. Schools operating as an integral part of the larger community
2. Collaboration and communication with families and community
3. Involvement of families and other stakeholders in school decision-making processes
4. The proposition that diversity can enrich the school
5. Families as partners in the education of their children
6. Using community resources to enhance the education of students

7. Informing the public
8. Schools and families keeping the best interests of children in mind

Standard 5: Acting with Integrity and Fairness, and in an Ethical Manner

A school administrator is an educational leader who promotes the success of all students and staff by acting with integrity and fairness, and in an ethical manner.

Performances
The administrator

1. Demonstrates a personal and professional code of ethics
2. Demonstrates values, beliefs, and attitudes that inspire others to higher levels of performance
3. Accepts responsibility for school operations
4. Considers the impact of one's administrative practices on others
5. Uses the influence of the office to enhance the educational program, rather than for personal gain
6. Treats people fairly, equitably, and with dignity and respect
7. Protects the rights and confidentiality of students and staff
8. Demonstrates appreciation for and sensitivity to the diversity in the school community after examining and considering the prevailing values
9. Recognizes and respects the legitimate authority of others
10. Welcomes and encourages the community into the school
11. Fulfills legal and contractual obligations
12. Makes decisions based on ethical implications within the spirit of the law

Knowledges
The administrator has a knowledge and understanding of

1. The purpose of education and the role of leadership in a changing society
2. The values, ethics, and challenges of the diverse school community
3. Professional codes of ethics

Dispositions
The administrator believes in, values, and is committed to

1. The ideal of the common good
2. The principles in the Bill of Rights
3. Bringing ethical principles to the decision-making process
4. Subordinating one's own interest to the good of the school community
5. Accepting the consequences for upholding one's principles and actions
6. Using the influence of one's office constructively and productively in the service of all students and their families
7. Development of a caring school community.

Standard 6: The Political, Social, Economic, Legal, and Cultural Context

A school administrator is an educational leader who promotes the success of all students and staff by understanding, responding to, and influencing the larger political, social, economic, legal, and cultural context.

Performances
The administrator facilitates processes to encourage that

1. The political, social, economic, legal, and cultural environment in which schools operate is influenced on behalf of students, their families, and staff
2. Communication occurs within the school community concerning trends, issues, and potential changes in the environment in which schools operate
3. There is the opportunity for ongoing dialogue with representatives of diverse community groups
4. The school community works within the framework of policies, laws, and regulations enacted by local, state, and federal authorities
5. Public policy is shaped to provide quality education for students
6. Lines of communication are developed with decision makers outside the school community

Knowledges
The administrator has a knowledge and understanding of

1. Principles of representative governance that support the system of American schools
2. The role of public education in developing and renewing a democratic society and an economically productive nation
3. The law as related to education and schooling
4. The political, social, cultural, and economic systems and processes that impact schools
5. Models and strategies of change and conflict resolution as applied to the larger political, social, cultural, and economic contexts of schooling
6. Global issues and forces affecting teaching and learning
7. The dynamics of policy development and advocacy under our democratic political system
8. The importance of diversity and equity in a democratic society

Dispositions
The administrator believes in, values, and is committed to

1. Education as a key to opportunity, social mobility, and self-realization
2. Recognizing a variety of ideas, values, and cultures
3. The importance of a continuing dialogue with other decision makers affecting education
4. Actively participating in the policy-making context in the service of education
5. Using legal systems to protect student, staff, and parental rights

STANDARDS FOR DISTRICT-LEVEL ADMINISTRATORS

Standard 7: Instructional Program (as used in Indiana)

A district administrator is an educational leader who guides, facilitates, and supports the success of all learners by providing leadership in curriculum development, learning assessment, instructional supervision, and program evaluation conducive to student learning, staff professional growth, and district accountability.

Performances
A district administrator facilitates processes and engages in activities that

1. Establish curriculum and instructional strategies to meet the needs of a diverse school community and its learners
2. Align curriculum with appropriate levels of learner development and styles
3. Involve appropriate faculty and community members in decision making regarding curriculum and special programs
4. Evaluate the use of resources, including technology, for effectiveness, equability, and relevance to the instructional process
5. Use test results and other assessments appropriately to improve the educational system

Knowledges
A district administrator has knowledge and understanding of

1. Development of core curriculum design and delivery systems for diverse school communities
2. Curriculum planning/futures, methods to anticipate occupational trends and their educational implication for lifelong learners
3. Instructional taxonomies, goals, objectives, and processes
4. Cognitive development and learning theories, and their importance to the sequencing of instruction
5. Child and adolescent growth and development
6. Processes to create developmentally appropriate curriculum and instructional practices for all learners
7. The use and role of computers and other technologies
8. Current trends and future learning needs
9. A process for faculty input in the continued and systematic renewal of the curriculum to ensure appropriate scope, sequence, and content
10. Curricular alignment to improve student performance and higher order thinking
11. The development, implementation, and monitoring of change processes to improve learning and climates for learning
12. Appropriate teaching methods and assessment strategies
13. Available instructional resources and how to use them in the most cost-effective and equitable manner
14. Applications of computer technology connected to instructional programs
15. Testing and alternative methods of assessment to evaluate learner achievement
16. A variety of instructional strategies based on current research

17. Student achievement monitoring and reporting systems
18. Diverse learner needs

Dispositions
A district administrator believes in, values, and is committed to

1. Developing and implementing a core curriculum design with instructional strategies that reflect multicultural sensitivity and learning styles
2. Using technology appropriately to enhance educational programming
3. Maintaining communication regarding curriculum among developmental levels and content areas
4. Using multiple assessment tools in determining the effectiveness of educational programs
5. Using multiple information sources for gathering perspectives from the educational community

Standard 8: Policy Implementation (as used in Indiana)

A district administrator is an educational leader who guides, facilitates, and supports the success of all learners by recommending and implementing policy that guides district operations.

Performances
A district administrator facilitates processes and engages in activities that

1. Maintain compliance with state, federal, and local laws and regulations
2. Promote positive relationships with the school board
3. Keep all staff current on applicable laws and regulations
4. Communicate all policies to staff and make them available to the greater school community

Knowledges
A district administrator has knowledge and understanding of

1. The system of public school governance in our democracy
2. The dynamics of superintendent–board of education roles and relationships
3. Conflict resolution skills
4. How to formulate sound district policy
5. Adapting local policy to accommodate state and federal regulations and requirements
6. Procedures to avoid civil and criminal liabilities
7. The contributions and benefits of professional organizations

Dispositions
A district administrator believes in, values, and is committed to

1. Working within the laws and regulations of state, federal, and local governments
2. Supporting the current fundamental system of the school system
3. Creating educational opportunities for the greater school community

APPENDIX B

Portfolio Exercise Scoring Rubric

The following is the scoring rubric to measure the level of attainment to the standards.

Level 5

The level 5 performance provides clear, compelling, and consistent evidence of the candidate's work to demonstrate attainment of the standard. There is clear and convincing evidence of the candidate's professional growth, as demonstrated through the description of the entry, the analysis of its importance, and the candidate's reflection on the activity. All components are tied together and show that the impact of the activity is relevant and worthwhile, and is part of a significant and meaningful plan for promoting the professional growth of the candidate and the improvement of the school and/or knowledge and practice of the education professionals within the school.

Level 4

The level 4 performance provides clear and consistent evidence of the candidate's work toward the attainment of the standard, to improve schools and to advance knowledge and practice of education professionals. There is clear and convincing evidence of the candidate's professional growth, as demonstrated through the description of the artifact, the analysis of the artifact's importance, and the candidate's reflection on the impact of the activity as well as future implications. In any or all of these areas, a level 4 performance may show imbalance or unevenness, but viewed as a whole, the piece provides clear evidence of the candidate's professional growth and understanding of the standard.

Level 3

The level 3 performance provides some evidence of the candidate's work to improve schools and advance knowledge and practice of education professionals through an understanding of the standard. Evidence is present of the candidate's professional growth, as demonstrated through the description of the artifact, the analysis of its importance, and the candidate's reflection on the impact of the activity as well as its impact on the future; however, such evidence may be less convincing, substantial, or significant. Analysis and/or reflection may be superficial and may lack depth.

Level 2

The level 2 performance provides limited evidence of the candidate's work to improve schools and advance knowledge and practice of education professionals through an understanding of the standard. Evidence of professional growth is limited. Evidence cited through description and analysis may be weak or skeletal, and/or reflection may be missing or unrelated to the description and analysis.

Level 1

The level 1 performance provides little or no evidence of the candidate's work to improve schools and advance knowledge and practice of education professionals through an understanding of the standard. There is little or no evidence of the candidate's professional growth. Description, analysis, and reflection may be unrelated to one another, may be so vague that they lack meaning, or one or more of these may be missing.

APPENDIX C

Additional Resources

NEW TEACHER AND MENTOR SUPPORT PROGRAMS

Boreen, J., Johnson, M., Niday, D., & Potts, J. (2000). *Mentoring beginning teachers: Guiding, reflecting, coaching.* York, ME: Stenhouse (www.stenhouse.com).

Brookfield, S. D. (1995). *Becoming a critically reflective teacher.* San Francisco, CA: Jossey-Bass (www.josseybass.com, 1-888-378-2537).

Brookfield, S. D., & Preskill, S. (1999). *Discussion as a way of teaching: Tools and techniques for democratic classrooms.* San Francisco, CA: Jossey-Bass (www.josseybass.com, 1-888-378-2537).

Buehl, D. (2001). *Classroom strategies for interactive learning.* Newark, DE: IRA (www.reading.org).

Burke, K. (1997). *Designing professional portfolios for change.* Arlington Heights, IL: SkyLight Training and Publishing (www.skylightedu.com, 1-800-348-4474).

Campbell, D., Cignetti, P., Melenyzer, B., Nettles, D., & Wyman, R. (2001). *How to develop a professional portfolio: A manual for teachers.* Boston: Allyn & Bacon (www.abacon.com).

Campbell, D., Melenyzer, B., Nettles, D., & Wyman, R. (2000). *Portfolio and performance assessment in teacher education.* Boston: Allyn & Bacon (www.abacon.com).

Costa, A., & Garmston, R. (1994). *Cognitive coaching: A foundation for Renaissance schools.* Norwood, MA: Christopher-Gordon Publishers.

Daniels, H., & Bizar, M. (1998). *Methods that matter: Six structures for best practice classrooms.* York, ME: Stenhouse Publishers (www.stenhouse.com).

Danielson, C. (2002). *Enhancing student achievement: A framework for school improvement.* Alexandria, VA: ASCD (www.ascd.org, 1-800-933-2723).

Danielson, C. (1996). *Enhancing professional practice: A framework for teaching.* Alexandria, VA: ASCD (www.ascd.org, 1-800-933-2723).

Danielson, C., & McGreal, T. (2000). *Teacher evaluation to enhance professional practice.* Alexandria, VA: ASCD (www.ascd.org, 1-800-933-2723).

Guskey, T. R. (2000). *Evaluating professional development.* Thousand Oaks, CA: Corwin Press (www.corwinpress.com).

Lyons, N. (Ed.). (1998). *With portfolio in hand: Validating the new teacher professionalism.* New York: Teachers College Press.

Martin-Kniep, G. O. (1999). *Capturing the wisdom of practice: Professional portfolios for educators.* Alexandria, VA: ASCD (www.ascd.org, 1-800-933-2723).

Pitton, D. (2000). *Mentoring novice teachers: Fostering a dialogue process.* Arlington Heights, IL: SkyLight Training and Publishing (www.skylightedu.com, 1-800-348-4474).

Podsen, I. J., & Denmark, V. M. (2000). *Coaching & mentoring: First-year & student teachers.* Larchmont, NY: Eye on Education (www.eyeoneducation.com, 1-914-833-0551).

Reeves, D. (1998). *Making standards work: How to implement standards-based assessments in the classroom, school, and district.* Denver, CO: Center for Performance Assessment (www.makingstandardswork.com).

Senge, P., Cambron-McCabe, N., Lucas, T., Smith, B., Dutton, J., & Kleiner, A. (2000). *Schools that learn: A fifth discipline fieldbook for educators, parents, and everyone who cares about education.* New York: Doubleday (www.fieldbook.com).

Wald, P. J., & Castleberry, M. S. (2000). *Educators as learners: Creating a professional learning community in your school.* Alexandria, VA: ASCD (www.ascd.org, 1-800-933-2723).

Wolf, K. (1999). *Leading the professional portfolio process for change.* Arlington Heights, IL: SkyLight Training and Publishing (www.skylightedu.com, 1-800-348-4474).

Zachary, L. J. (2000). *The mentor's guide: Facilitating effective learning relationships.* San Francisco, CA: Jossey-Bass (www.josseybass.com, 1-888-378-2537).

Zemelman, S., Daniels, H., & Hyde, A. (1998). *Best practice: New standards for teaching and learning in America's schools.* Portsmouth, NH: Heinemann (www.heinemann.com).

PORTFOLIO

Boreen, J., Johnson, M., Niday, D., & Potts, J. (2000). *Mentoring beginning teachers: Guiding, reflecting, and coaching.* York, ME: Stenhouse Publishers.

Burke, K. (1997). *Designing professional portfolios for change.* Arlington Heights, IL: SkyLight Training and Publishing.

Campbell, D., Cignetti, P., Melenyzer, B., Nettles, D., & Wyman, R. (1997). *How to develop a professional portfolio: A manual for teachers.* Boston: Allyn & Bacon.

Campbell, D., Melenyzer, B., Nettles, D., & Wyman, R. (2000). *Portfolio and performance assessment in teacher education.* Boston: Allyn & Bacon.

Lyons, N. (Ed.). (1998). *With portfolio in hand: Validating the new teacher professionalism.* New York: Teachers College Press.

Pitton, D. E. (2000). *Mentoring novice teachers: Fostering a dialogue process.* Arlington Heights, IL: SkyLight Training and Publishing.

Wolf, K. (1999). *Leading the professional portfolio process for change.* Arlington Heights, IL: SkyLight Training and Publishing.

ACTION RESEARCH

Dillon, D. (2000). Kids insight: *Reconsidering how to meet the literacy needs of all students.* Newark, DE: IRA.

Glanz, J. (1999). Action research. *Journal of Staff Development, 20*(3), 22–23.

Hubbard, R., & Power, B. (1999). *Living the questions: A guide for teacher-researchers.* York, ME: Stenhouse.

Richardson, J. (2000). *Tools for schools.* Oxford, OH: NSDC.

Sagor, R. (1992). *How to conduct collaborative action research.* Alexandria, VA: ASCD.

BEST PRACTICES

Daniels, H., & Bizar, M. (1998). *Methods that matter: Six structures for best practice classrooms.* York, ME: Stenhouse.

Martin–Kniep, B. (2000). *Becoming a better teacher: Eight innovations that work.* Alexandria, VA: ASCD.

Marzano, R., Pickering, D., & Pollock, J. (2001). *Classroom instruction that works: Research-based strategies for increasing student achievement.* Alexandria, VA: ASCD.

Zemelman, S., Daniels, H., & Hyde, A. (1998*). New standards for teaching and learning in America's schools.* Portsmouth, NH: Heinemann.

PROFESSIONAL GROWTH

Brookfield, S. (1995). *Becoming a critically reflective teacher.* San Francisco, CA: Jossey-Bass.

Brookfield, S., & Preskill, S. (1999). *Discussion as a way of teaching: Tools and techniques for democratic classrooms.* San Francisco, CA: Jossey-Bass.

Burke, K. (1997). *Designing professional portfolios for change.* Arlington Heights, IL: SkyLight Training and Publishing.

Campbell, D., Cignetti, P., Melenyzer, B., Nettles, D., & Wyman, R. (2001). *How to develop a professional portfolio: A manual for teachers.* Boston: Allyn & Bacon.

Campbell, D., Melenyzer, B., Nettles, D., & Wyman, R. (2000). *Portfolio and performance assessment in teacher education.* Boston: Allyn & Bacon.

Danielson, C. (1996). *Enhancing professional practice: A framework for teaching.* Alexandria, VA: ASCD.

Danielson, C., and McGreal, T. (2000). *Teacher evaluation to enhance professional practice.* Alexandria, VA: ASCD.

Ginsberg, M., & Wlodkowski, R. (2000). *Creating highly motivating classrooms for all students: A schoolwide approach to powerful teaching with diverse learners.* San Francisco, CA: Jossey-Bass.

Graves, D. (2001). *The energy to teach.* Portsmouth, NH: Heinemann.

Kohn, A. (1998). *What to look for in a classroom.* San Francisco, CA: Jossey-Bass.

Martin–Kniep, G. (1999). *Capturing the wisdom of practice: Professional portfolios for educators.* Alexandria, VA: ASCD.

Payne, R. (1998). *A framework for understanding poverty.* Baytown, TX: RFT Publishing.

Steeves, K., & Browne, B. (2000). *Preparing teachers for national board certification: A facilitator's guide.* New York: Guilford Press.

Wolf, K. (1999). *Leading the professional portfolio process for change.* Arlington Heights, IL: SkyLight Training and Publishing.

REFERENCES

AASPA (American Association of School Personnel Administrators), (1988). *Standards for school personnel administrators*. Virginia Beach, VA: Author.

Alexander, K., & Alexander, M. D. (1998). *American public school law*. 4th ed. Belmont, CA: Wadsworth.

Alexander, K., & Alexander, M. D. (2001). *American public school law*. 5th ed. Belmont, CA: Wadsworth.

Andrews, R. L., & Soder, R. (1987). Principal leadership and student achievement. *Educational Leadership, 44*(6), 9–11.

Ansari, W. E. (2003). Educational partnerships for public health: Do stakeholders perceive similar outcomes? *Journal of Public Health and Management Practice, 9*(2), 136–156.

Arter, J. (2001). Learning teams for classroom assessment literacy. *NASSP: Bulletin, 85*(621), 53–63.

Bagin, D., & Gallagher, D. R. (2001). *The school and community relations*. Boston: Allyn & Bacon.

Balch, B. V. (2003). District accreditation—Implementation considerations for aligning greatness. *Journal of School Improvement, 4*(1), 1–5.

Barnard, C. (1938). *The functions of the executive*. Cambridge, MA: Harvard University Press.

Barth, R. (1995). *Improving schools from within*. San Francisco, CA: Jossey-Bass.

Bass, B. M. (1985). *Leadership and performance beyond expectations*. New York: Free Press.

Beerman, S. E., & Kowalski, T. J. (1998). Program change and administrative roles in Indiana's school-to-work pilot site high schools. *Contemporary Education, 69*(2), 73–79.

Bennis, W. (1995). The 4 competencies of leadership. In D. A. Kolb, J. S. Osland, & I. M. Rubin (Eds.), *The organizational behavior reader* (pp. 395–401). Upper Saddle River, NJ: Prentice Hall.

Bennis, W., & Nanus, B. (1985). *Leaders: The strategies for taking charge*. New York: Harper & Row.

Blanck, G. (1984). *Vigotski: Memoria y vigencia*. Buenos Aires: Cultura y Cognicion.

Blasé, J., & Blasé, J. R. (1999). Instructional leadership through the teachers' eyes. *High School Magazine, 6*, 17–20.

Bolman, L. G., & Deal, T. E. (1991). *Reframing organizations: Artistry, choice and leadership*. San Francisco, CA: Jossey-Bass.

Bolman, L. G., & Deal, T. E. (1995). *Leading with soul*. San Francisco, CA: Jossey-Bass.

Bolman, L. G., & Deal, T. E. (1997). *Reframing organizations: Artistry, choice, and leadership*. San Francisco, CA: Jossey-Bass.

Bray, M. (2003). Community initiatives in education: Goals, dimensions and linkages with governments. *Compare, 33*(1), 31–45.

Brimley, V., & Garfield, R. (2002). *Financing education in a climate of change*. Boston: Allyn & Bacon.

Burns, J. M. (1978). *Leadership*. New York: Harper & Row.

Callahan, R. E. (1962). *Education and the cult of efficiency*. Chicago: University of Chicago Press.

Charlotte Advocates for Education (2004). *Community guide to understanding the school budget*. Retrieved March 21, 2004 from www.publiceducation.org/pdf/MemPubs/CMS_Guide_School_Budget.pdf

Chute, E. (1999). *Good principals need a wide array of skills*. Retrieved September 13, 2002 from www.post-gazette.com/regionstate/1999082Train7.asp.

Clarke, S. R. P. (2000). The principal at the centre of reform: Some lessons from the field. *International Journal of Leadership in Education, 3*(1), 57–73.

Cole, M. (1996). *Cultural psychology: A once and future discipline*. Cambridge, MA: Harvard University Press.

Colon, R. (1989). Issues brought to grievance arbitration by Iowa public schoolteachers: January 1982 through December 1986. *Journal of Collective Negotiations in the Public Sector, 18*(3), 217–227.

Colon, R. (1990). Job security issues in grievance arbitration—what do they tell us? *Journal of Collective Negotiations in the Public Sector, 19*(4), 243–251.

Cooney, S., Moore, B., & Bottoms, G. (2002). Gaps to close to prep them for high school. *The Education Digest, 67*(8), 44–46.

Cooper, B. S., Fusarelli, L. D., & Randall, E. V. (2004). *Better policies, better schools: Theories and applications*. Boston: Pearson.

Cordeiro, P. A., Reagan, T. G., & Martinez, L. P. (1994). *Multiculturism and TQE: Addressing cultural diversity in schools.* Thousand Oaks, CA: Corwin Press.

Cordeiro, P. A. (1999). The principal's role in curricular leadership and program development. In L. W. Hughes (Ed.), *The principal as leader* (pp. 131–153). New York: Macmillan.

Council of Chief State School Officers (1996). *Interstate school leaders licensure consortium standards for school leaders.* Washington, DC.

Cunningham, W. G., & Gresso, D. W. (1993). *Cultural leadership: The culture of excellence in education.* Boston: Allyn & Bacon.

Cunningham, W. G., & Cordeiro, P. A. (2000). *Educational administration: A problem-based approach.* Boston: Allyn & Bacon.

Danielson, C. (2002). *Enhancing student achievement. A framework for school improvement.* Alexandria, VA: ASCD.

Darling–Hammond, L. 1999. Target time toward teachers. *Journal of Staff Development 20*(2), 31–36.

Davis, S. (2001). Notable quotes: Spotlight on principals. *Leadership, 30*(3), 6.

Deal, T. E., & Peterson, K. D. (1999). *Shaping school culture: The heart of leadership.* San Francisco, CA: Jossey-Bass.

DeCenzo, D. A., & Silhanek, B. (2002). *Human relations: Personal and professional development.* 2nd ed. Upper Saddle River, NJ: Prentice Hall.

Dempster, N. (2001). *The professional development of school principals: A fine balance.* Retrieved July 29, 2003 from www.griffith.edu.au/centre/clme/publications/extra files/proflecture.pdf.

Dionne, E. J., Jr. (1991). *Why Americans hate politics.* New York: Simon and Schuster.

Downton, J. V., Jr. (1973). *Rebel leadership: Commitment and charisma in the revolutionary process.* New York: Free Press.

DuFour, R. (1999). Teaching teams need specific support from the sidelines to each top performance. *Journal of Staff Development 20*(2), 57–58.

DuFour, R. (2002). The learning-centered principal. *Educational Leadership, 59*(8), 12–15.

DuFour, R. (2003). Leading edge: Are you looking out in the window or in the mirror? *Journal of Staff Development, 25*(3), 36–37.

DuFour, R., & Eaker, R. (1998). *Professional learning communities at work: Best practices for enhancing stu-dent achievement.* Bloomington, IN: National Educational Service.

Edmonds, R. R. (1979). Effective schools for the urban poor. *Educational Leadership, 37*(1), 15–23.

Edmonds, R. R. (1982). On school improvement. *Educational Leadership, 40*(2), 12–15.

EdSource (1998). School principals: What do they really want? *Thrust for Educational Leadership, 27*(7), 4.

Education Finance Statistics Center (2004). *National Center for Education Statistics.* Retrieved March 15, 2004 from http://nces.ed.gov/edfin.

Essex, N. L. (2002). *School law and the public schools: A practical guide for educational leaders.* 2nd ed. Boston: Allyn & Bacon.

Evans, R. (1996). *The human side of school leadership.* San Francisco, CA: Jossey-Bass.

Federal News Service (2001, February). *Leadership for student learning: Restructuring school district leadership.* Washington, DC, Institute for Educational Leadership.

Fullan, M. G. (1991). *The new meaning of educational change.* 2nd ed. New York: Teachers College Press.

Fullan, M. G. (1993). *Change forces.* New York: Falmer Press.

Fullan, M. G. (1998). Leadership for the 21st century: Breaking the bonds of dependency, *Educational Leadership, 55*(7), 6–11.

Fullan, M. G. (2001). *Leading in a culture of change.* San Francisco, CA: Jossey-Bass.

Fullan, M. G. (2003). *The moral imperative of school leadership.* Thousand Oaks, CA: Joint Publication, Corwin Press & Ontario Principal Council.

Garfield, R., Garfield, G., & Willardson, J. D. (2003). *Policy and politics in American education.* Atlanta, GA: St. Barthelemy Press.

Giles, S., & Giles, D. E. (1990). *Superintendent turnover: Crisis facing California school districts.* Washington, DC: Office of Educational Research and Improvement. (ERIC Documentation Reproduction Service No. ED325981).

Glatthorn, A. A. (1997). *Differentiated supervision.* Alexandria, VA: ASCD.

Glickman, C. D. (1991). Pretending not to know what we know. *Educational Leadership, 48*(8), 4–10.

Green, R. L. (2001). *Practicing the art of leadership. A problem-based approach to implementing the ISLLC standards.* Columbus, OH: Prentice-Hall.

Gregory, G. H. (2003). *Differentiated instructional strategies in practice: Training, implementation, and supervision.* Thousand Oaks, CA: Corwin Press.

Griswold, D. (1992). Public relations news. In D. L. Wilcox, P. H. Ault, & W. K. Agee (Eds.). *Public relations strategies and tactics* (pp. 7–10). New York: Harper-Collins.

Grossman, D. (1995). *On killing: The psychological cost of learning to kill in war and society.* Boston: Little, Brown.

Hanvey, R. (1982). An attainable global perspective. *Theory Into Practice, 21*(3), 162–167.

Harris, T. (2001). How urban schools are solving the principal shortage. *Principal, 18,* 10–11.

Heifetz, R. A. (1994). *Leadership without easy answers.* Cambridge, MA: The Belknap Press of Harvard Press.

Herzberg, F. (1993). *The motivation to work.* New Brunswick, NJ: Transaction.

Holliday, A. E. (1988). In search of an answer: What is school public relations? *Journal of Educational Public Relations, 11,* 10–17.

Hosley, C. A., Gensheimer, L., & Yang, M. (2003). Building effective working relationships across culturally and ethnically diverse communities. *Child Welfare, LXXXII*(2), 157–168.

Hopkins, G. (2002, March). *Teachers urged to consider principalship.* Retrieved September 13, 2002 from www.educationworld.com/aadmin/admin262.shtml.

Hord, S. (1998). *Creating a professional learning community: Cottonwood Creek School.* Washington, DC: Office of Educational Research and Improvement. (ERIC Document Reproduction No. ED424685).

Hoy, W. K., & Miskel, C. G. (1987). *Educational administration.* New York: Random House.

Huer, M. B., & Saenz, T. I. (2003). Challenges and strategies for conducting survey and focus group research with culturally diverse groups. *American Journal of Speech-Language Pathology, 12,* 209–220.

Indiana Professional Standards Board (2004). *District Leader Standards.* Retrieved March 23, 2004 from www.in.gov/psb/Standards/DistrictAdminContStds.html.

Interstate School Leaders Licensure Consortium (2000). *ISLCC projects and participating states.* Retrieved May 20, 2002 from www.ccsso.org/pdfs/isllcchart00.pdf

Jantzi, D., & Leithwood, K. (1996). Toward an explanation of variation in teachers' perceptions of transformational school leadership. *Educational Administration Quarterly, 32,* 512–538.

Johnson, S. M. (1996). *Leading to change: The challenge of the new superintendency.* San Francisco, CA: Jossey-Bass.

Johnson, S. M., Kardos, S. M., Birkeland, S. E., Kauffman, D., Liu, E., & Peske, H. G. (2001). Retaining the next generation of teachers: The importance of school based support. *Harvard Education Letter* (July/August), 1–2.

Kidder, R. M. (2003). Eat right, cheat less: Profiling the honest teen. *Institute for Global Ethics: Ethics Newsline, 6*(16), 1.

Killion, J. (2005). Staff development guide. *Principal Leadership, 5*(5), 53–54.

Kleinginna, P. R., & Kleinginna, A.M. (1981). A categorized list of emotion definitions with suggestions for a consensual definition. *Motivation and Emotion 5*(4), 345–359.

Lacey, P. (2005). *Caught in an inescapable network of mutuality.* Proceedings of the Eyes Wide Open Exhibit, American Friends Service Committee, Washington, DC. Retrieved April 1, 2005 from www.afsc.org/eyes/mlk-remarks.htm

Lambert, L. (1998). *Building leadership capacity in schools.* Alexandria, VA: ASCD.

Larson, C. L., & Ovando, C. J. (2001). *The color of bureaucracy. The politics of equity in multicultural school communities.* Belmont, CA: Wadsworth/Thomson Learning.

Lunenburg, F. C., & Ornstein, A. C. (2000). *Educational administration: Concepts and practices.* 3rd ed. Belmont, CA: Wadsworth.

Marion, R. (2002). *Leadership in education: Organizational theory for the practitioner.* Upper Saddle River, NJ: Prentice-Hall.

Marriott, D. (2001, September). Managing school culture. *Principal,* 75–77.

Marzano R. (2003). *What works in schools: Translating research into action* (p. 76). Alexandria, VA: ASCD.

Maslow, A. (1970). *Motivation and personality.* Rev. ed. New York: Harper & Row.

Mays, G. P., Halverson, P. K., & Scutchfield, F. D. (2003). Behind the curve? What we know and need to learn from pubic health systems research. *Journal of Public Health Management Practice, 9*(3), 179–182.

McGregor, D. (1960). *The human side of the enterprise.* New York: McGraw-Hill.

McKay, G. (1999, August). *Back to school: A matter of principals.* Retrieved September 13, 2002 from www.post-gazette.com/regionstate/19990822principal1.asp.

Ménendez–Morse, S. (1992). *Leadership characteristics that facilitate change.* Southwest Educational Development Laboratory. Retrieved March 15, 2004 from www .sedl.org/publs/catalog/items/cha02.html.

Messer, D. (2001). *The impact of dismissal of non-tenured teachers on principals in Tennessee: A dissertation.* Retrieved July 29, 2003 from http://etd-submit.etsu. edu/etd/theses/available/etd-0820101-094517.

Moll, L. C. (2000). *Vygotsky and education.* New York: Cambridge University Press.

Murtadha Watts, K., & Larson, C. (1999). *Toward a socially critical theory of womanist leadership.* Paper presented at the annual meeting of the American Educational Research Association, Montreal, Canada.

National Association of Child Advocates (2003). *Selection process for child advocacy issues and strategies.* Retrieved December 28, 2002 from www.childadvocacy .org/childtxtS.html.

National School Boards Association (2003). School board policies. *National School Boards Association website.* Retrieved July 29, 2003 from www.nsba.org/site/index.asp.

National School Public Relations Association. (1985). *Evaluating your school PR investment.* Arlington, VA: Author.

O'Laughlin, J. (2001). Recruitment: A comprehensive approach. *Leadership, 30*(1), 14–16.

Ovando, C. J., & Collier, V. P. (1998). *Bilingual and ESL classrooms: Teaching in multicultural contexts.* Boston: McGraw-Hill.

Owens, R. G. (1987). *Organizational behavior in education.* Englewood Cliffs, NJ: Prentice Hall.

Pasi, R. J. (2001). A climate for achievement. *Principal Leadership, 2*(4), 17–20.

Peterson, K. D. (2002). Positive or negative. *Journal of Staff Development, 23*(3), 1.

Peterson, K. D., & Deal, T. E. (1998). How leaders influence the culture of schools. *Educational Leadership, 56*(1), 28–30.

Peterson, K. D., & Deal, T. E. (2002). *Shaping school culture fieldbook.* San Francisco, CA: Jossey-Bass.

Print, M., & Coleman, D. (2003). Towards understanding of social capital and citizenship education. *Cambridge Journal of Education, 33*(1), 123–149.

Public Agenda (2001). *Trying to stay ahead of the game: Superintendents and principals talk about school leadership.* New York: Wallace Reader's Digest Funds.

Razik, R. A., & Swanson, A. D. (2001). *Fundamental concepts of educational leadership.* Upper Saddle River, NJ: Prentice Hall.

Reeder, W. G. (1944). *School boards and superintendents.* New York: Macmillan.

Reitzug, U. C. (1994). A case study of empowering principal behavior. *American Education Research Journal, 31,* 283–307.

Reitzug, U. C., & Burrello, L. C. (1995). How principals can build self-renewing schools. *Educational Leadership, 52,* 48–50.

Richardson, J. (2001, April/May). Educator, know thyself: Learning where you are is the first step in establishing your direction. *Tools for Schools.* Oxford, OH, National Staff Development Council, 1–4.

Roe, W. (1961). *School business management.* New York: McGraw-Hill.

Roethlisberger, F., & Dickson, W. (1939). *Management and the worker.* Cambridge, MA: Harvard University Press.

Sagor, R. (2000). *Guiding school improvement with action research.* Alexandria, VA: ASCD.

Santiago v. Paterson Board of Education, Passaic County, C01-03 (New Jersey School Ethics Commission, July, 2003). Retrieved July 29, 2003 from www .state.nj.us/njded/legal/ethics/00-03/c0103.pdf.

Schein, E. H. (1984). Coming to a new awareness of organizational culture. *Sloan Management Review, 25*(2), 3–16.

Senge, P. M. (1994). *The fifth discipline: The art and practice of the learning organization.* New York: Doubleday.

Sergiovanni, T. J. (1984). Leadership and excellence in school. *Educational Leadership, 41,* 4–13.

Sergiovanni, T. J. (1992). *Moral leadership: Getting to the heart of school improvement.* San Francisco, CA: Jossey-Bass.

Sergiovanni, T. J. (1997). *Value-added leadership: How to get extraordinary performance in school.* 2nd ed. New York: Harcourt Brace.

Sergiovanni, T. J. (1999). *The lifeworld of leadership: Creating culture, community, and personal meaning in our schools.* San Francisco, CA: Jossey-Bass.

Sergiovanni, T. J. (2001). *The principalship. A reflective practice perspective.* 4th ed. Boston: Allyn & Bacon.

Sergiovanni, T. J., Burlingame, M., Coombs, F. S., & Thurston, P. W. (1992). *Educational governance and administration.* Paramus, NJ: Prentice Hall.

Seyfarth, J. T., & Nowinski, E. M. (1987). Administrator feedback can improve classroom instruction. *NASSP Bulletin, 71,* 47–50.

Shakeshaft, C. (1989). *Women in educational administration*. Newbury Park, CA: Sage.

Sheppard, B. (1996). Exploring the transformational nature of instructional leadership. *Alberta Journal of Educational Research, 42,* 325–344.

Simon, H. (1947). *Administrative behavior*. New York: The Free Press.

Sobel, D. S., & Ornstein, R. (1996). *The healthy mind healthy body*. New York: Time Life Medical.

Soto, G., Huer, M., & Taylor, O. (1997). Multicultural issues in augmentative and alternative communications. In L. Lloyd, D. Fuller, & H. Arvidson (Eds.). *Augmentative and alternative communication* (pp. 406–413). Boston: Allyn & Bacon.

Stein, M. (1998). *High performance learning communities District 2: Report on year one implementation of school learning communities. High performance training communities project*. Washington, DC: Office of Educational Research and Improvement. (ERIC Document Reproduction No. ED429263).

Stroll, L., & Fink, D. (1994). School effectiveness and school improvement: Voices from the field. *School Effectiveness and School Improvement, 5*(2), 149–177.

Swanson, A. D., & King, R. A. (1997). *School finance: Its economics and politics*. 2nd ed. New York: Longman.

Tomlinson, C. A., & Allan, S. D. (2000). *Leadership for differentiating schools & classrooms*. Alexandria, VA: ASCD.

Weeks, R. H. (2001). Managing legal affairs. *School Business Affairs, 67*(1), 4–11.

Wink, J., & Putney, L. (2002). *A vision of Vygotsky*. Boston: Allyn & Bacon.

Zaleznik, A. (1989). *The managerial mystique: Restoring leadership in business*. New York: Harper & Row.

Zionts, L. T., Zionts, P., Harrison, S., & Bellinger, O. (2003). Urban African American families' perceptions of cultural sensitivity within the special education system. *Focus on Autism and Other Developmental Disabilities, 18*(1), 41–50.

INDEX